The
QUIET
Rise of
INTROVERTS

*8 Practices for Living and
Loving in a Noisy World*

Brenda Knowles

MJF BOOKS
New York

Published by MJF Books
Fine Communications
589 Eighth Avenue, 6th Floor
New York, NY 10018

The Quiet Rise of Introverts
LC Control Number: 2018963883
ISBN 978-1-60671-448-5

BG   10   9   8   7   6   5   4   3   2   1

"Go to the gym, meditate, but learn to reach for the people you love." —**Dr. Sue Johnson**

For my parents and children, who taught me about perspective, courage and love.

CONTENTS

AUTHOR'S PREFACE

If you are most comfortable dwelling in your inner world, exploring thoughts, ideas and feelings, then integrating relationships into your life can be a challenging and scary prospect. You feel safe in solitude. You recharge best alone; yet, you want closeness, companionship, and love.

Many introverts struggle to find the energy and courage to engage in the swirl of socializing and the responsibilities of relationships. Those who do enter into relationships often find themselves choosing between their need for space and their partner's need for intimacy.

What if, as an introvert, you could maintain the natural inclinations of your personality and develop meaningful relationships? What if there was a guide to move you through a maturity continuum that could result in a balance of inner satisfaction and outer connection?

The eight practices found in this book serve as that guide. A progression of awareness and action steps will help you move past the anxiety and stress of living an ill-fitting extroverted life, through the important but insufficient goals of independence and self-reliance, and to the secure and fulfilling state of authenticity and deep connection with others.

The intention of this book is not to turn introverts into extroverts.

The intention is to teach introverts how to be both pro-self and pro-relationship. Pro-self, meaning that we have a good grasp of personal values, personality traits, past wounds, and the bravery necessary to advocate for all of them. Pro-self does not mean placing blame on others. For example, "He never listens and it is destroying our marriage," puts the onus on one partner. That statement is not *pro-self*. A mature and *pro-relationship* stance would look like, "We have trouble listening to and understanding each other. It is taking a toll on our marriage."

I AM WITH YOU

As an introvert and highly sensitive person, I understand the need for non-critical, nonjudgmental support and encouragement. I know the intimate fears and perceived inferiority of the introverted individual.

I spent many hours playing by myself in my room as a child, while my extroverted sister sought and received attention from my parents. I obtained a business degree and forced my quietly observant personality to become vocally active in corporate America. I married an extroverted and aggressive man to help navigate the bold and busy world.

At age thirty-five, I began listening to my internal voice. I started giving it credence. I began to value my introverted nature rather than suppress it to keep up outgoing and energized appearances. At age forty-two, I found myself divorced and back in the dating world.

The divorce and my newfound appreciation for my inner world served as catalysts for my deep dive into research and writing regarding relationships and temperaments.

As a personal and relationship coach, as well as a longtime writer and researcher on the subject of the deeply introspective and sensitive lifestyle, I learn and share along with my clients and readers. I have experienced the life-changing benefits of growth-fostering relationships.

One question I asked myself post-divorce, and one you might consider as an introvert is, "Is it more satisfying to be independent or interdependent?"

GROWTH AND MATURITY LEADING TO CONTENTMENT

In personal growth, there is a maturity continuum. This continuum moves us from *dependence* on others to *independence* and reliance on ourselves, and to *interdependence* or a balanced state of self within relationships.

Independence exists within interdependence; therefore, it is possible to experience the fulfilling interaction of the two. We can honor our autonomy (as introverts love to do) and honor the warmth of healthy relationships as well.

INTRODUCTION:
SAFE IN SOLITUDE

The Quiet Rise of Introverts: 8 *Practices for Living and Loving in a Noisy World* seeks to show introverts how to reduce anxiety and create interdependence in their lives. It is organized with the maturity continuum in mind.

Each chapter explains a challenge within the introvert's growth process. The practice described in each chapter provides relief for those challenges. Tangible action steps at the end of each section help you apply the solution to everyday living and loving.

The book starts with a look at the pressure we feel to mold our personalities to align with the *extrovert ideal*. We are dependent on the approval of others, so we conform. Wearing an extroverted mask takes a toll on our energy reserves and our self-esteem, often causing anxiety and depression.

To alleviate the stress of living falsely, we must strive for independence from the extroverted identity. We have to take the time and space to gain self-awareness and appreciation.

- **Practice One** helps the introvert deal with the challenges of the loud, rapid-paced culture we live in. Slowing down allows us to pay attention and hear the voice within us, dying to give direction

- **Practice Two** offers knowledge and tips to help calm our nervous system without feeling guilty. Introverts tend to have easily stimulated nervous systems. A challenge we often face is a feeling of selfishness if we spend too much time in self-care

- **Practice Three** teaches the reader how to be true to himself or herself in the inner and outer world—how to confront our character weaknesses, develop self-discipline, and take action to express ourselves

Practices four through eight take us outside of our comfort zone. They move us from self to self plus other, from independence to interdependence.

- **Practice Four** helps us move past our belief that it is weak to need others. It is OK to rely on others, beneficial even

- **Practice Five** shows us how to face and even embrace conflict. In this chapter, we see how pain teaches us about ourselves and confrontation sparks growth

- **Practice Six**, like practice two, focuses on the nervous system, but practice six teaches us how to calm our partner's nervous system rather than our own. We rise to the challenge of maintaining a high level of responsiveness within our relationship

- **Practice Seven** moves us from interactions with our small circle of family and friends to the larger venue of community. We explore how to contribute to the world and cultivate purpose, without running out of energy

- Lastly, **Practice Eight** is a lesson in lifelong maintenance and curiosity that leads to a balance of inner and outer worlds for the introvert. It is a practice of creating harmony with others without forgetting ourselves

If you feel pulled between your need for solitude and other's need for your presence and attention, this book will help you. You will gain understanding, insight, and applicable action steps by following the maturity process outlined within its pages. It is possible to be an introvert within healthy and secure relationships.

SECTION I:
DEPENDENCE

Extroverts, Anxiety, and the Maturity
Continuum

The acclaimed Swiss psychiatrist, Carl Jung, first introduced the terms *introvert* and *extravert* in 1921 in his groundbreaking book, *Psychological Types.* Jung described extraversion and hence the extravert, as characterized by,

"...interest in the external object, responsiveness, and a ready acceptance of external happenings, a desire to influence and be influenced by events, a need to join in and get "with it," the capacity to endure bustle and noise of every kind, and actually find them enjoyable, constant attention to the surrounding world, the cultivation of friends and acquaintances, none too carefully selected....

The psychic life of this type of person is enacted, as it were, outside himself, in the environment. He lives in and through others; all self-communings give him the creeps."

In contrast, an introvert, according to Jung, was primarily focused on the inner world of the psyche. The introvert,

"... holds aloof from external happenings, does not join in, has a distinct dislike of society as soon as he finds himself among too many people. In a large gathering he feels lonely and lost.... His own world is a safe harbour, a carefully tended and walled-in garden, closed to the public and prying eyes.... His relations with other people become warm only when safety is guaranteed, and when he can lay aside his defensive distrust. All too often he cannot, and consequently the number of friends and acquaintances

is very restricted...His best work is done with his own resources, on his own initiative, and in his own way."

Jung did not consider the introvert a social loss. To him, introverts were not rejecting the world but instead seeking quietude where they could best make their contribution to the community.

Susan Cain, author of *Quiet: The Power of Introverts in a World That Can't Stop Talking*, points out that introverts and extroverts also differ in the amount of stimulation they prefer. Introverts work better with lower levels of stimulation. Their brains and nervous systems process sensory information differently. They are more sensitive to it.

Although we may not think of people as stimuli, they are. Interactions with people are stimulating, particularly to introverts if they occur in a large group or with people who are not close companions.

It should be noted that according to decades of Myers Briggs Type Indicator data, introversion and extroversion reside on a continuum within each of us. We all have introverted and extroverted tendencies, but usually one temperament is more natural or preferred.

THE EXTROVERT IDEAL

For several reasons, it is widely believed in Western cultures that life as an extrovert is better than life as an introvert.

One of these reasons is the notion that gregarious personalities fare better when competing for jobs, friends, and mates. As mentioned by Susan Cain in *Quiet*, this line of thought gained momentum in the early twentieth century. At that time, the United States was moving from a rural agricultural economy and population to more urban industrial ways of living. People migrated from small farm towns to bigger cities in search of manufacturing jobs and steady paychecks.

Among strangers in a new city, anonymity encouraged bold behavior. Your family's reputation, as well as your own, were not known or on the line. The risk of running into your coworkers at church or the local store was smaller. Emboldened by anonymity and the need to stand out among the competition, people transformed themselves from soft-spoken farmers into confident speakers with solid eye contact. If they didn't, there would be fewer employment opportunities and successes. They would not be positioned in upwardly mobile and well-thought-of social circles. They would not attract and secure the best or richest mate.

SMALL RURAL COMFORT

Much like those rural wallflowers prior to their move to the big cities, I experienced the bliss of living in a small, agriculturally based town in the middle of Michigan. My high school class numbered fewer than 250 students. My dad owned the local shoe store, and many of my friends' parents grew up in this same small town. Everybody knew each other. My family and I lived "in the country" on a dirt road. It was quiet in our little house, nestled between a creek and fields that farmers rotated annually between soybeans and corn.

The small school and community afforded us a sense of belonging without having to compete for everything. There were socioeconomic differences among the town's people, but overall the playing field seemed level. Everyone played their parts and worked together to support the community.

Hindsight tells me one reason for this cohesiveness: the fact that everyone knew where you lived, who you were related to and where you worked. Our proximity kept everyone in check. It was damn difficult to exist in anonymity. Harmony was the name of the game, and a sharing of resources kept things running smoothly. Granted, there were only a handful of stores for everyone to shop. Fewer resources could incite competition, but mostly it offered a chance to catch up with your neighbor if you ran into them at the bank or meat market. The experience was pleasant rather than frustrating. So many people lived in a small, quiet neighborhood or out in the rural areas (like I did) that we welcomed a chance run-in with someone we knew. We weren't constantly burdened with crowds, traffic, long lines or job scarcity.

I personally had a wonderful balance of quiet country living and active social experiences. At home in our small farmhouse, there was an absence of hustle and bustle. There was a cat or two stretched out on the porch, breezes rustling through the leaves of walnut and pear trees, little to no traffic on our dirt road, comforting aromas coming from the oven, and glorious solitude in my upstairs corner bedroom. When "in town" or at school activities, I could be found hanging out in the basement of my friends' homes watching movies, sharing stories, or playing cards with anywhere from one to fifteen people. As teens, my friends and I spent a lot of time "cruising" in our cars looking for (and often finding) boys and parties. There were school functions like dances and football games too. I was never a big fan of group sleepovers, but I endured and even enjoyed them, knowing I would be home in my own, peaceful bedroom the next night.

But, even in this idyllic atmosphere, I was fed a steady diet of television shows and movies that presented city living and brash lifestyles as the way to go. I thought all of the possibilities and fulfilling careers were to be found in bigger, more alive cities. Surely, the people in the city were more interesting, intellectual and exciting.

My sleepy little town could not keep me. By the time I graduated from high school, I was convinced my small community was holding me back.

COMPETITION AT HOME

There was another factor motivating me to move out of my hometown. Although, I did not feel competition among my classmates, friends or coworkers (during my years employed by Kentucky Fried Chicken and my dad's shoe store), I did feel significant competition and inferiority at home.

My mom, dad, and sister were all extroverts. Although I am sure my parents' outgoing personalities subconsciously affected my view of my nature, it was my younger sister's strong and vocal personality and others' responses to it that most influenced my self-perception: namely, that it was better to be a boisterous, center-of-attention type than a quiet, sensitive remain-on-the-sidelines type.

The new city dwellers of the 1920s learned to stand out from their peers by adopting high-voltage personalities and a willingness to be the proverbial squeaky wheel. My sister was born with those skills. And they worked for her. She garnered the enviable and fun nicknames of "imp," "character," and "pistol." It was hard not to notice her. It was also hard to get noticed when around her.

As a tender-hearted, read-in-her-room, play-with-dolls, kind of child, I had to really stretch myself to stand out. As teenagers, my sister and I both had a lot of friends, but she played team sports, was on the homecoming court, and was never without a boyfriend. I did not lack for social activities. I was a pom-pom girl and had a circle of six or more close girlfriends. I felt safe in these groups. I had the occasional short-term boyfriend. I was not a standout, but I was happy, except when compared to my sister.

WHY EXTROVERSION IS ADMIRED

Extroverts still hold the top seat for ideal personality, although introverts have gained ground in the last few years, thanks to Susan Cain's book, a positive correlation between the Internet and introvert skills, and a new appreciation by everyone for downtime and solitude due to their rareness in this frenetic world.

One reason society still prefers the extroverted personality type is the perceived and proven idea that extroverts are more financially successful. In February of 2015, Truity Dyometrics did a survey regarding career income and personality type. Personality type was determined by answers to the survey and their correlation with the sixteen MBTI (Myers–Briggs Personality Indicator) types. According to the results, extroverted types (those with an E as the first letter of their four-letter Myers–Briggs code) made the most money and coincidentally managed the most people. Extroverts are more apt to take managerial positions, which often earn larger salaries.

Salary isn't everything, though! The Truity questionnaire also revealed that job satisfaction did not correlate with greater income.

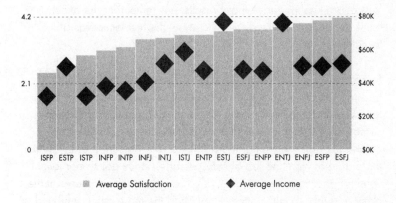

JOB SATISFACTION VS. INCOME AMONG THE 16 PERSONALITY TYPES[6]

Charisma and the ability to influence others with overt communication are two qualities deemed by the general public as representative of leaders. Leaders earn more money.

This is not to say introverts are not effective leaders. Two separate studies facilitated by Wharton Business School professor and author Adam Grant and two colleagues, professor Francesca Gino of Harvard Business School and professor David Hofman of the Kenan-Flagler Business School at the University of North Carolina, showed introverts to be the most effective managers or leaders of innovators and self-directed employees. Introverted leaders are more apt to listen to their subordinates, stay open to suggestions, and grant them autonomy. This ultimately results in superior outcomes.

Employees looking for direction fare better with extroverted leaders. Extroverted leaders inspire action in passive employees.

I took the Myers–Briggs Personality Type Indicator test for the first time as a young twentysomething working for office furniture manufacturer Steelcase as a sales administrator. Much to my frustration, I neither have those results, nor remember the exact four-letter code I received, but I do know the first letter was an I, for Introversion.

Surrounded by humorous and outgoing salespeople, I did my best to keep my scarlet letter to myself. I wanted the coveted *E* for extrovert because *E* meant well-liked, fun, popular, and even successful. *I* meant forever in the shadows as the administrator behind the higher-earning, more striking salesperson. It didn't matter that I did not want the job of salesperson—I once got so nervous, I vomited prior to a face-to-face walk-through with the end-user at the close of a job. It only mattered that I had the more quiet, inhibited personality type that most likely would not rise very high in the corporate standings.

Even today, in a seemingly introvert-friendly culture permeated with technologies that allow us to "connect" via the Internet and texting, the pace and quantity of connections feels more extroverted than introverted. Traditionally introverted careers, such as writing, require social media presence and repeated exposure of the public to you and your work. Authors must develop marketing platforms or *branding* to showcase their writing, style, and persona. I've seen a hierarchy of introvert writers and social media personalities develop based on their number of followers and their social media presence. Those introverted authors who more aggressively market themselves, engage in more collaborative projects, and present lively personalities edge out the traditionally introspective authors.

As an introverted writer, it's difficult for me to watch colleagues reach and announce 100,000 followers on Facebook and market yet another webinar for the masses. It almost feels like a betrayal of our type and, at the same time, makes me feel like I am falling behind. Why can't I promote and publish as much as Author A? The answer is that I don't have the time or energy to do that. My introverted nature has reached its maximum output between running a household, parenting, coaching, writing, and maintaining an intimate relationship. My social energy is cooked.

DOES EXTROVERSION EQUAL HAPPINESS?

Several studies claim extroversion correlates with happiness. Who doesn't want maximum happiness in their life? But how is happiness defined in these studies?

In a study titled "The Happiness of Extroverts," done by Michael Argyle and Luo Lu of Oxford University in 1990, happiness was found to have three components:

1. Frequency and degree of positive affect, or joy; 2. The average level of satisfaction over a period; and 3. The absence of negative feelings, such as depression and anxiety. These components can be shortened to positive affect, satisfaction, and the absence of distress.

The Oxford study of 130 subjects focused on the subjects' level of extroversion and their effects of joy and satisfaction. Introverts were simply defined by their absence of extroverted traits, primarily the reduction or absence of social interactions and activities.

Data was collected on happiness, social activities, and personality (extroversion–introversion) via the Oxford Happiness Inventory (OHI), a social activity scale which inquires about enjoyment and frequency of participation in activities with varying levels of interactions, i.e. "taking a long bath", "a quiet chat with a friend," or "going to the pub," and the extroversion scale from the EPQ

(Extended Project Qualification, a test taken pre-university in the United Kingdom, similar to the SAT or a more subjective equivalent).

Introverts were found to withdraw more from social situations and extroverts were found to be happier than introverts. Gender was not a significant factor, except that females were found to enjoy party settings more than males. An interesting point found in the study was that merely judging an activity as enjoyable did not correlate with happiness. Participation did correlate with happiness. The biggest predictor of unhappiness? Withdrawal from social activities. The more withdrawal, the bigger the effect on your happiness, principally the less happiness experienced.

The Oxford study gave two explanations for the results that extroverts are generally happier than introverts: 1. Extroverts engage in more social activities, which enhances happiness; and 2. Introverts withdraw more from social situations, which reduces happiness.

The study further declared that participation in social activities predicts happiness, independent of extroversion or introversion. This indicates that introverts could be happier if they participated in more social engagements. It is not their personality that holds them back or the extrovert's personality that propels them ahead in happiness levels. The biggest takeaway here is that the avoidance of social activities significantly decreases happiness.

One question that arose from the correlational study was whether happiness was a by-product of extroverted behavior or extroverted behavior was a by-product of happiness. Could the causation go both ways? That is, could a happy introvert engage in more extroverted behavior and create a positive feedback loop of happiness? And what is happiness, anyway?

In a *Psychology Today* article titled "Are Extroverts Really Happier?" PhD assistant professor of psychiatry Arnie Kozak looks at happiness through the introvert's lens. He states that correlations between extroversion and happiness are based on how extroversion is measured. Studies do not measure positively valued introvert qualities or, in some cases, the absence of inherent extroversion. Kozak asks us to look at pioneering positive psychologist Martin Seligman's facets of happiness, represented in the acronym PERMA: Positivity, Engagement, Relationships, Meaning, and Accomplishment. In Seligman's version of happiness, if we find meaning in an activity or idea, we do not have to strive for extroverted types of happy experiences. Positive emotions flow, with or without socializing.

Dr. Kozak reminds us of the contentment or equanimity the Buddha exhibited. The Buddha remained peaceful, regardless of the outer environment. Introverts have access to rich inner experiences (as do extroverts, but they do not experience the same energy boost). If we expand our definition of happiness beyond a high-arousal, extrovert-dominated one, and include low-arousal, introvert-based feelings (contentment, peacefulness, calm, appreciation), the correlations to happiness change.

A comment on Dr. Kozak's article brought up an interesting difference between extroverts and introverts. The commenter said introverts don't necessarily prefer less time in groups (socializing), but are more focused with their interests and relationships. When in groups or relationships that advance their interests, and make efficient use of their time, introverts are happy.

DEPENDENCE PORTION OF THE MATURITY CONTINUUM

When speaking of the maturity continuum—dependence > independence > interdependence—Stephen R. Covey, author of the classic leadership and personal success book, *The 7 Habits of Highly Effective People*, said, *"Dependence is the paradigm of you—you take care of me; you come through for me; you didn't come through; I blame you for the results."*

At the dependence maturity level, the locus of control is in other's hands. Just as physical dependence requires others to care and provide sustenance for us, intellectual dependence demands that others think and make decisions for us. If we are emotionally dependent, we lean on others to elevate our moods and give us a sense of security and self-worth. As individuals in the dependence stage, we believe our self-worth is determined by what others think of us.

For introverts, that often means we undervalue our nature because the external community values high-energy, friendly, fun, talkative, outgoing, popular people. It often means we adjust our demeanor to align with the external world's expectations. We put on our active, vocal, group-focused masks and carry on.

As an adult, I chose a business degree from a large university instead of the English literature teaching degree I initially considered. In my mind, a bold business career in corporate America trumped a bookish, introspective career in academia. The potential for a high salary was greater, and honestly, the corporate world seemed like a confident and more successful person's choice. I admired those with business aspirations and abilities so much that I married a Finance major who later earned an MBA.

His personality lived up to my revered extroverted expectations. He spoke quickly and with conviction. He thrived on completion. I was in awe. He garnered a very high salary to go with his high-powered personality. He represented the extrovert ideal.

The perspective that extroversion is the ideal is pervasive in our culture.

I've seen well-meaning suburban moms set up bonfire parties and sleepovers for their daughters, who, much to their mother's dismay, want to stay in their room and read or watch videos.

My client, *Carrie* (not her real name), once told me of a time when she and her sister were at a bar and met a few men who worked in marketing for a big corporation. Carrie was also in marketing. Although the men would never guess it, she was also a true introvert. She dazzled them with her smile, witty stories, and confidence. Carrie's sister even commented admiringly about how "on" and outgoing Carrie was at the bar. The men found her and her sister so engaging they invited them to their company Christmas party that night. Carrie went to the party. Once there, she found herself in group discussions where everyone had to answer questions like, "What is your favorite Christmas memory?". This on-the-spot questioning gave *Carrie* a little anxiety—introverts often find off-the-cuff speaking challenging—but she answered with rousing cheers from the group. She knew she had won them over.

The next day Carrie felt "gross" and out-of-sorts, and it wasn't because she drank too much at the party. She had put on a heavy extroverted mask the day before and now her spirit was flagging. She had charmed everyone but left her real self out in the cold. She felt so low and misrepresented she began to question whether she could stay in the marketing business.

This constant reconciling of the outer world with our true inner world, takes a toll on introverts.

ANXIETY AND INTROVERTS

Often the result of constant reconciling is anxiety. Anxiety is both an emotion and a clinical condition.[1] The emotion anxiety is natural. Anxiety is predicting or preparing for a negative outcome to a future situation. While waiting for results from a medical biopsy, we experience anxiety. While driving to a first date, sweaty palms or butterflies in the stomach are normal. Simply feeling anxious is not a major cause for concern. According to Dr. Rob Lamberts, MD, in his article, "How Can You Tell If You Have Anxiety?," two things separate the emotional state of anxiety from the clinical condition: duration and severity. To officially diagnose someone with clinical anxiety, the symptoms must significantly affect the daily life of the individual and must have existed for at least three months. However, Dr. Lamberts admits that most cases are diagnosed prior to three months.

A common definition of emotional anxiety is a feeling of powerlessness and helplessness. If we cannot control something that could potentially harm us, we feel anxious. In clinical anxiety, *life* feels out of control. It is possible to feel anxious about feeling anxious, which compounds clinical anxiety.

Many introverts report feeling overwhelmed or lost in rumination when they experience excessive stimulation and too many pulls on their attention. Since introverts are energy conservers who rejuvenate by spending quiet time with their thoughts, ideas, and feelings, they get drained when forced to focus on many external influences. They experience racing mind, where thoughts run like bullet trains through their brains. This causes physical lethargy, where their bodies feel heavy and their ability to speak declines. They may express extra emotions. If they are not able to recover in low-stimulation settings, their energy diminishes and they feel out of control. Too much stimulation quickly leads to anxiety for an introvert.

It should be noted that anxiety—both the emotion and clinical condition—can wreak havoc on our physical as well as our mental health. For example, if we feel stress every day after lunch when our new, short-tempered boss goes over our work with a fine-toothed comb, we may start to suffer from digestive problems. Our boss's critical eye and short fuse become perceived threats to that primitive part of our brain which still prepares for saber-toothed tiger attacks, hence setting in motion the fight-or-flight response. When under threat, our brain sends a message to our gut to slow down its digestive process, so that we can focus blood flow to the extremities (arms and legs), in case we have to fight or flee.

Anxiety can appear as an enduring, non-specific worry or dread, which is called generalized anxiety disorder (GAD), or it can appear in episodic flare-ups such as with a panic disorder or phobia. According to Dr. Lamberts, these kinds of anxiety call for professional help, but other methods of attenuating anxiety's symptoms are:

- Not feeling ashamed. We do not choose to experience anxiety. It's the result of genetic sensitivity and environmental influences

- Looking for root causes. Usually something in our past has not been resolved. Understanding why we feel the way we do is a step toward healing

- Talking to someone. If the anxiety is manageable, then talking with a trusted friend, family member, or religious leader might help. A professional is recommended if your anxiety affects day-to-day living

- Taking medication. Under the guidance of a professional, short- or long-term medication can be helpful. Short-term medications, like Valium, are addictive. If they are needed more than a few times a week, long-term daily options are suggested

SOCIAL ANXIETY

Sometimes anxiety centers on interactions with others, as is the case with social anxiety disorder. Social anxiety is the fear of social or performance situations in which embarrassment, judgment, criticism, or rejection are perceived to be dangers. Performance can mean something as simple as speaking up during a group project. Social anxiety and shyness go hand in hand.

Social anxiety is all too familiar to many introverts. Is there a difference between introversion and social anxiety disorder? Yes. Dr. Ellen Hendriksen, clinical psychologist at Boston University's Center for Anxiety and Related Disorders, says there are four differences:

1. Like introverts, the socially anxious crowd has a genetic predisposition toward its traits, but there are two other influences. The first is that we learn that we do not measure up to scrutiny. Perhaps we had a fretful parent who always worried about what the neighbors thought, or an older sibling who over-powered us at every turn. Somehow, we learned that we are always being judged and found lacking.

The second key ingredient to social anxiety is avoidance. We intentionally miss out on social interactions. We go to the store late at night to avoid running into anyone we know. We leave parties early or don't attend at all to stave off the potential of saying something embarrassing.

In contrast, introversion is primarily a part of our inherent personality. We are born with the genetic trait and the brain processes unique to introverts, such as extra blood flow to the parts of the brain responsible for remembering, solving problems, and planning.

2. A fear of revealing a flaw or vulnerability. In social anxiety, we think there is something wrong with us. If we socialize too much, someone may discover the chink in our armor. In order to avoid judgment, we play it small and keep our presence unobtrusive. If we don't stand out, we won't get picked on. The truth is these flaws are only legitimate to us. Most people would not consider them an issue. Dr. Hendriksen gives appearance as an example of a perceived flaw. Perhaps we think we will turn beet red when all eyes are on us (and people will care), or we were always the "ugly" sister and fear being picked on for our looks. Fears of looking stupid or incompetent are also perceived defects that hold back those with social anxiety. Introversion alone may make us prefer to listen more than talk, but this is not out of a fear of revealing something about us that could permanently damage our self-worth.

Social anxiety may fluctuate depending on the audience. Close and trusted companions may free the socially anxious to be themselves and to contribute. Strangers may cause the anxious to withdraw in fear of making a mistake or not knowing what to say. Acquaintances and coworkers may require the socially anxious to develop a false persona.

The creation of a social persona/self helps many people identify and participate within a group. Some call it their "game face" or their "work smile." It helps them feel a sense of belonging; however, the social self, if too removed from the true self, feels extra heavy and draining.

Perfectionism rears its ugly head in social anxiety. The only way to prevent harsh criticism is to be perfectly witty, charismatic, beautiful, and smart. The pressure to not make mistakes paralyzes us. For example, we may decline a friend's invitation to try out a new yoga class because we are afraid we won't be able to do the poses and others will make fun of us.

The non-socially-anxious do not feel every interaction is a do-or-die performance. They don't beat themselves up if they forget someone's name or deliver a dull response to a question. They give themselves permission to make mistakes, and they believe others will forgive them too.

3. Social anxiety gets in the way of living our life. When fear drives our behavior, we miss out on what others have to offer. We skip events, we avoid social interaction. And even when we *are* physically present, we are mentally absent because we are focused on what could go wrong. Remember the Oxford University study we talked about earlier? This kind of social avoidance is associated with lower happiness levels

Introversion is distinct from clinical social anxiety. Introverts may leave parties early or stay home in the first place, but they choose to do so. They could spend time talking and joking with friends at the party, but they prefer to have a nice, quiet dinner at home with their significant other. It is a preference not a fear that drives their decisions.

SOCIAL ANXIETY DISORDER AND CHEMICAL DEPENDENCY

A study called the "Oregon Depression Project" followed the lives of 1709 adolescents until their thirtieth birthdays (although many participants dropped out before they hit thirty). The study showed a correlation between social anxiety and alcohol and marijuana *dependency*, but no correlation between social anxiety and alcohol and marijuana *abuse*.

Drug abuse is an intense desire to use increasing amounts of a particular substance to the exclusion of other activities. Drug dependence is the body's physical need for a specific agent; dependency and addiction are the same thing.

After controlling for theoretically relevant variables such as the presence of other anxiety disorder diagnoses and previous substance use dependencies, the correlation between a lifetime history of social anxiety disorder (SAD) and a lifetime history of alcohol and marijuana dependency remained.

According to an article on Susan Cain's website *Quiet Revolution* by Dr. Hendriksen titled, "Hope in a Bottle: The Link Between Alcohol and Social Anxiety", the socially anxious turn to *liquid courage* to quell their social inhibitions. Alcohol serves a few purposes for the socially afraid. It loosens them up before the party and gives them the courage to even attend the shindig. Once at the event, alcohol serves as the magic elixir that makes them fun, entertaining and relaxed. Alcohol also helps the socially anxious drown their sorrows and mellow their memories after a perceived failed night of mixing and mingling. "I should not have said that!" "What was I thinking wearing the bright pink sweater? I stood out like a pink elephant."

Especially troubling is that although people with SAD drink less overall than other, non-SAD people, their incidence of hazardous drinking with negative consequences was much higher. Their infrequent attendance of social functions keeps their alcohol consumption low overall, but when they do imbibe, they go all out. The heavy exposure, low tolerance, and inexperience put them in danger of risky behavior such as indiscriminate sex or failure to show up for work.

Many of the plaguing hallmarks of SAD—fear of not living up to scrutiny, fear of revealing a flaw, perfectionism—come out at parties. Alcohol and/or drugs ameliorate a person's perceived social shortcomings. It isn't long before a person with SAD believes he or she needs the mood-altering drug to fit in at all, hence the resulting dependency.

Interestingly, the definition of SAD found in the DSM-IV (*Diagnostic and Statistical Manual of Mental Disorders*) does not include the avoidance of social activities. Without this criterion, sufferers of SAD appear to experience greater incidents of alcohol use dependency. The avoidance criterion in the DSM-III definition kept the SAD individuals who did not attend as many social events (they avoided them) in the calculations, thus reducing the numbers associated with increased risk of lifetime alcohol dependence.

BREAKING THE BARRIER OF SOCIAL ANXIETY

We all experience awkward social moments and those moments when our hearts pound out of our chests. I have a particularly strong reaction—immediate perspiration, flushing of the face—when I feel I am being oserved. If a conversation suddenly swings so that all eyes are on me, it is not uncommon for me to forget where I was going with my dialogue. Times from my childhood when my sister pounced on an error in my speech or made fun of my contribution to the conversation still haunt me. But I am happy to say (yes, I'm a happy introvert) that such moments do not hold me back from taking part in the world. I enthusiastically put myself out into the mix of socializing, loving and learning.

Here are a few of the action steps I've employed myself and recommend to push past the barrier of social anxiety:

1. Leave your comfort zone. Home is so nice and safe because it either holds people you know well or offers solitude with no people at all. If you leave the comfort zone of your home, however, you can find and forge new places where you can have social interactions without feeling emotionally unsafe. The key to finding an encouraging and kind atmosphere is to think about what you love to do. Do you get a rush from exercising? Join a group class that includes music you enjoy. Most classes meet regularly. You will see the same people every week. They will become familiar and, as a bonus, they also love fitness and the same type of music. Maybe you want a more serene setting than the gym. How about a writing class or a guitar lesson, which combine solitary practice, one-on-one coaching, and group workshops or performances? I have personally used these two settings to launch myself into new social circles and increase my repertoire of skills, although the guitar lessons proved more of a boon for making like-minded friends than for becoming a musical talent. Take small but committed steps. If you sign up for a class and pay for it, chances are you will follow through. I chose a writing class for beginners in a part of the city where I didn't know anyone. I often find it easier to try new skill-building activities among strangers. If I do make a mistake, I won't run into my new classmates at the grocery store or my kids' schools. Much like the rural farm people who

moved into the city for industrial jobs in the early 1900s, I am emboldened by anonymity. Once in a new place with new people, I take the time to notice how I feel. Am I energized? Do I feel safe to make mistakes? If the answer is yes, I dig in deep and buoy my social strength by slowly increasing my participation. For example, I may ask the teacher or a fellow participant a question after class.

2. Ask questions. Most people are experts on themselves, so ask open-ended questions about their lives and interests. A simple, "What do you love to do in your free time?" can easily garner a few minutes of conversation. Note that this question is unintimidating and that there are no right or wrong answers, so even other socially anxious introverts will find it easy to respond. Other examples of safe and conversation-generating questions are, "So you are from Chicago. What do you miss about that city?" or "How did you meet your boyfriend/ husband/girlfriend/wife?" In her book, *If You Want to Write: A Book about Art, Independence and Spirit*, Brenda Ueland says that most people will find you extremely charming and witty if you ask questions about them. Bonus: there is no fear of revealing too much if you're the one asking questions.

3. Volunteer or help someone. I've been a part of several volunteer organizations. Who can fault, make fun of, or complain about someone who is volunteering his or her time? Again, pick an area that interests you—child welfare, education, cancer research, animal rescue, etc.—and dip your toe in. Commit to attending at least three sessions. Giving to others feels good and puts you in environments with other generous, thoughtful people. Volunteers tend to be unintimidating, open-minded, and open-hearted people. I have seen introverts take on jobs at friends' parties, such as stocking the food table or cleaning up afterwards. The sense of purpose and focus gives them the ability to take part in the event and even stay longer than planned.

4. Make socializing manageable. Invite one or two people out for lunch. Approach people one at a time. Introverts are usually more comfortable in one-on-one settings. Even at a neighborhood BBQ, it is possible to get a neighbor alone on the edge of the gathering and discuss subjects near and dear to you. If you are especially brave, attend an event by yourself. You look more approachable to others if you are alone. I started attending church by myself, and found I was quite popular at the coffee hour afterward. I enjoyed the service part of church, which allowed me to be in my head and relatively anonymous, but then was able to circulate in small doses with one or two people afterward. Gaining the friendship of people at a manageable pace—one or two at a time—works perfectly for introverts and making one new friend often leads to introductions to more new friends.

The eight practices outlined in the following chapters will expand on and provide additional methods of alleviating the anxiety that introverts experience while living and loving in an extroverted world.

SECTION II:
INDEPENDENCE

Stephen Covey said that independence is the paradigm of *I*. "*I* can do it; *I* am responsible; *I* am self-reliant; *I* can choose." After passing through the dependent stage of the maturity continuum, we hone skills to get what we want ourselves, rather than depending on others to do it for us. We physically do the work ourselves. We mentally think and make decisions for ourselves. We emotionally validate ourselves from within. We self-direct and act on our own accord instead of reacting to the stimuli of others.

We may think we've left dependency in the dust, but, we often have emotional dependencies. The immature or insensitive behavior of others still controls our reactions. We still take on a victim mentality and complain about the state of our lives, blaming others for our misfortune.

A way to test whether we are stuck in dependency is to change our circumstances and see if unhappiness persists. A dependent individual remains unhappy or returns to an unhappy state relatively quickly, if they are not truly inner-directed.

Independence is not the same as individualism. Individualism conjures up "do your own thing" images of liberated and somewhat self-centered people. Independence, for our purposes, is a close relative of autonomy. Along with mastery and purpose, autonomy is one of the three basic human needs, according to motivation and self-determination theorists Edward Deci and Richard Ryan. If we want to motivate a human, we should give him or her autonomy, something to master and the opportunity to be part of something bigger than him or herself.

Our current culture values independence (and sometimes individualism) and deplores anything that smacks of neediness or dependence. *You are complete on your own. You don't need a man/woman! Pick yourself up by the bootstraps!* Even though educational and professional settings emphasize group projects (introvert nightmares) and collaboration, independence is still revered. We reward and praise those who think independently and make decisions quickly. We see them as smart.

In parenting, the goal of most parents is to teach their children how to live on their own, each maturity stage taking the kids further and further away from home. This may, however, be changing. A 2014 Pew study of recent housing trends found that more 18–34-year-olds live with their parents than either on their own or with a significant other. But despite the statistics, living in your parent's home still carries a certain stigma.

Inner direction is a leg up maturity-wise, compared to being externally directed. It requires the wherewithal to act on our own, regardless of circumstances and others' opinions. Although independence is more mature than dependence, it is still missing the key element of relating to others. Independence does provide the necessary foundation for interdependence though, which we will discuss in Section III.

As introverts move along the maturity continuum, we move further away from dependency on our parents and society's view of us. No longer do we blame others for our misfortunes or give them credit for our successes. It's all on us now. The paradigm of "I" replaces the paradigm of "You." Because we are more self-directed, we examine our lives and figure out what we need to feel successful in our own way. When we know ourselves, it is easier to be morally and soulfully articulate. It is easier to both advocate for and accept ourselves.

As we fuel the flames of independence, we figure out who we are, what we need, how to take care of ourselves, and how to be our best selves.

THE PURPOSE OF EACH PRACTICE

Each of the following chapters introduces a practice and principles that support it. The purpose of each practice is to help the reader become more effective and fulfilled in everyday living. Applying the practices and using the principles as guidance help you reduce anxiety and feel the energy and ease of living meaningfully, while moving along the maturity continuum.

Practice One: Waking Up Principles of Self-Awareness

"What lies before us and what lies behind us are small matters, compared to what lies within us." —Henry S. Haskins, "Meditations on Wall Street"

IS IT TIME TO TWEAK THE RECIPE?

I like to have a recipe. I can make anything with a recipe. I'm not afraid to try exotic dishes or difficult techniques, as long as they are spelled out. I could follow the instructions of an old-world Italian lady and make fabulous *gnocchi*, but I would beg her to write down the steps so that I could make it on my own later.

Recipe following is how I've lived much of my life. "Combine 1 college education with 1 caring and successful husband. Add 3 children and stir." This turned out well for the presentation part, but flopped in the end.

Who knew ingredients could evolve? Who knew we'd eventually feel limited by *a recipe?*

Ultimately, winging it became necessary; a random combination of internal and external mixing led to a completely different, but richer, end product.

SHARING RECIPES

In the beginning, my husband and I even had recipes to follow and share with our children. We had access to oodles of child-rearing books and we ate them up. We deferred to *Consumer Reports* for the correct stroller, crib, monitor, etc. We controlled and extolled proper procedures for all aspects of feeding, sleeping, pooping, learning, and disciplining. If by some miracle there wasn't a book on the subject we needed, we looked to our family, friends, and neighbors to provide examples and instructions. This was all fine and dandy, until the first time we were confronted with a child who didn't fit the textbook description. Who knew recipes could go rogue?

"If we expect our children to always grow smoothly and steadily and happily, then...we're going to worry a lot more than if we are comfortable with the fact that human growth is full of slides backward as well as leaps forward, and is sure to include times of withdrawal, opposition, and anger, just as it encompasses tears as well as laughter." —**Fred Rogers**

VAPID BETTY CROCKER

Sometimes as a meticulous recipe follower, I'd forget to taste the food at the end of production. I was so sure the recipe was foolproof, I assumed the food would be delicious or as good as the last time I made it. This was a mistake. We need to periodically taste and tweak our creations.

Ten years and three children into my marriage, this textbook homemaker was one depressed tuna casserole. I needed zing, pizzazz, brightness of flavor. I was making sloppy joes like a robot. They were consistently tasty, but I was bland. My heart was heavy. So, there I was with a house full of people counting on me to be Betty Crocker, and I couldn't even be me—because I didn't know what I was made of.

WHAT AM I? MASHED POTATOES?

What if I was *just a follower* or *tasteless mashed potatoes?* I was unsure how and if I wanted to look inward within myself. I did know that I couldn't bear to make one more uninspired hot dish. I could not let myself become stale living at *sous chef* status. I was simmering away to nothing in a very un-Martha Stewart way (unless Martha snaps at her kids, feels mediocre, and cries in the shower).

So, I timidly stepped outside my own kitchen and experienced the full flavor of someone else's sloppy joes. I smelled the aroma of *coq au vin* and noted its essence. I gathered enough spicy ingredients (in my case, fitness training, guitar lessons, writing) to ensure my own depth of flavor. I made renegade chef friends: either people who had been burned and learned, or had always made up their own concoctions (or both!). They gave me the freedom to wreck a few meals. Dared me to fail or completely kick a recipe up a notch. Wham!

WINGING IT

It turns out that I'm capable of winging it, even if I prefer not to. I have imagination and, what's more, I can teach others to make their own *gnocchi*. I'll even write it down for them, but it's better if they just give it a whirl themselves. It doesn't matter if the cake doesn't rise or the soup is salty. Trial and error is the risk-taking/transformative part, the part where our lives and hearts rise above the container. Where internal goes external, with a dash of creativity.

As for my kids, we still confer with friends and family regarding their upbringing because it is fun, and because they often reassure us that there is no such thing as a foolproof child manual. We try to let the kids develop their own flavors. I know they need help and guidelines, but I also know they need to taste what life has to offer, beyond the laminated recipe card. I want them to know there are recipes out there, but that it's perfectly wild and delicious to sample a lot before choosing a menu. They need permission to experiment and mess up. They need encouragement to be who they are without a recipe. They need to know what they are made of.

I first wrote what you've just read above as an essay years ago when my marriage was coming to a close, but my self-awareness was blossoming. It shows the first step toward independence: waking up. If you are "making sloppy joes like a robot" or raising your children just like your neighbors raise theirs, you may be sleepwalking. You may be completely unconscious regarding who you are. I was.

FITTING IN BUT LOSING OUT

The Swiss psychiatrist Carl Jung spent the first nine years of his life as an only child. He lived primarily in his imagination, and blissfully engaged in hours of solitary play. When he started school, he found he could not remain connected with his beloved inner world. In order to fit in, he adapted to his new school companions—and in doing so, he felt that he lost an important part of himself.

Many introverts can relate to Jung's story. In order to fit in, we abandon the sweet sense of home found in our thoughts and feelings and move along with the current of our culture and social circles. Often this means making ourselves into something we are not, including rowdy playmates, perpetually industrious parents, and vapid Betty Crockers.

THE COMPETITIVE MERITOCRACY

We all (introverts and extroverts alike) let the hum and busy-ness of external life lull us into a complacent stupor. In fact, *New York Times* columnist David Brooks says in his book, *The Road to Character*, if you've lived in the last sixty or seventy years, you've been living in a competitive *meritocracy*. This means that you've lived with a lot of competition and pressure regarding individual achievement. Doing well in school, getting into the right college, finding a great job, and moving toward success have been focuses for you. Comparing yourself to others has been the primary gauge for determining whether you are "doing it right."

Brooks uses the term *"résumé virtues"* to denote the skills that we bring to the job market and those that contribute to external success. Internal virtues, such as kindness, faithfulness, bravery, and honesty, are what Brooks calls "*eulogy* virtues" —these are the qualities people remember us for after we're gone. Just like the personality traits of introversion and extroversion, we all have résumé and eulogy virtues, but one is usually more pronounced than the other.

The education system (as well as society in general) orients itself around résumé virtues. It's a lot easier to articulate and plan career goals and skills than it is to describe and execute a plan for profound moral character.

With all our time, energy, and attention focused on external achievement, we have less time, energy, and attention to put toward our inner realm. It's easier to keep on following the recipe and be an achievement automaton than it is to pause and reflect on what we are doing and who we are.

Because our inner world is so neglected and the inner world is the introvert's happy place, the introvert suffers. It's difficult to go against the current, without the electricity of our inner world to energize us.

Conflict is stimulating too. It's easier to maintain harmony by complacently agreeing than it is to find the vocabulary and energy to speak to the contrary of cultural norms.

Carl Jung said personality or wholeness is an achievement earned (not given) in the second half of life. The first half of life is spent emancipating ourselves from our parents, finding a spouse, creating a family, and becoming an effective contributor. Jung's theories about the first half of life line up with the meritocracy ideals. After we've satisfied these ideals, we look inward. We develop our psychological selves by noticing tensions within us. We pull opposite traits into closer balance: for example, if we are more introverted, we might strengthen our extroverted skills. We bring the unconscious into the conscious. Jung called this process *individuation*, and we will discuss it further in Practice Three.

In my own life, I've followed the pattern or recipe Jung described. As a suburban, stay-at-home mom, I fell into the trance of the ultra-achiever. I kept myself and our three children so busy there was no time to think. My outwardly successful husband led the show. He attended a highly accredited MBA program. He had a high-paying salary as a portfolio manager at a hedge fund. He was doing it right according to the meritocracy and society at large. We were perfect citizens—buying cars and homes and saving for our kids' college funds and our retirement.

I did not take the time to question our lifestyle or to look inward until I was thirty-seven years old. Perched on the ledge between the first and second halves of my life, my eyes fluttered open and self-awareness slipped in.

TENSION

The first feeling that interrupted my sleep was a low-grade tension. The year my children were six, four, and two, I found myself at the doctor's office sitting in a vulnerably thin examination gown, asking for something to give me energy, boost physical desire, and stave off depression. The doctor wrote a prescription for Prozac, an antidepressant.

At that point in my life, I had a part-time nanny, personal trainer, housecleaners, and virtually no budget restrictions. There were no reasons why I should not be able to design and juggle magnificent schedules, or to have profoundly happy children, a well decorated home, and a blissful demeanor. And yet I found myself being short with the kids, emotionally overwrought, and just plain sad. I had no drive. I tuned out some of the noise and requests of me in order to get through the day. I vacillated between extreme sensitivity and dull malaise.

There was tension between the roles I played and the real me. I did not know it at the time, but I was living the perfect life for an extroverted commercial success. The life of the competitive external achiever (a successful individual, according to the meritocracy) did not sit well with my internal temperament. My husband and I had engineered a world where I had no time alone, few generative conversations, and a constant outpouring of energy. Many people would say that's the life of a parent. I agree. The point I hope to make is that my situation caused enough dissonance within me to make me seek relief.

But I subconsciously knew that the doctor could not fix my problems (dependent paradigm). I had to work on them myself. I'd effectively contributed, as Jung said, and now it was time to look inward.

I did not fill the prescription.

SOLITUDE

My love affair with solitude began. Instinctively, I searched for time and space to be alone. I had a desperate need to regain energy. Socializing with the neighbors and dinners with my husband's coworkers did not recharge me. Only in solitude could I breathe. In solitude thoughts were heard, daydreams flowed, clarity arose, ideas came together. *I* came together.

The problem was that when I spent time alone, I was not spending time with my family. Good mothers don't spend time away from their families. They live to be with their children. It was hard to explain to my husband why I would rather read for two hours by myself than be with him.

"I had told people of my intention to be alone for a time. At once I realized they looked upon this declaration as a rejection of them and their company. I felt apologetic, even ashamed, that I would have wanted such a curious thing as solitude, and then sorry that I had made a point of announcing my desire for it." —Doris Grumbach, *Fifty Days of Solitude*

It seemed other people loved the constant hits of interaction through social media, emails, texts, phone calls, and in-person meetings. Everybody wanted to keep in touch all the time. My former in-laws called frequently for short conversations. Quite often the calls felt like interruptions to any rare moments of concentration I had.

Why was it so vital for me to be left alone? What was wrong with me? For a long time, I could not articulate what my soul needed.

Slowly, with intentional observance, I began to notice that if I did not take time for myself, my presence became muddled. My thoughts gridlocked and my demeanor was zombie-like. I came across as *there but not there.* That was not good enough.

Many people come alive in relationships. The more the better. I was driven by relationships, but found myself inspired and transcendent in solitude.

Eventually, I stumbled upon Marti Olsen Laney's classic introvert guide, *The Introvert Advantage.* I took the included assessment to find out if I had introverted traits such as:

- When I need a rest, I prefer time alone or with one or two close people rather than a group

- When I work on projects, I like to have larger, uninterrupted time periods rather than smaller chunks

- I can zone out if too much is going on

- I don't like to interrupt others; I don't like to be interrupted

- I can become grouchy if I am around people or activities too long

- I often dread returning phone calls

- I am creative/imaginative

- I form lasting relationships

- I usually need to think before I respond or speak

I answered yes to the majority of them. What a revelation! I had to know more. I read anything I could find on introversion in 2008, before Susan Cain had popularized the topic by writing her book, *Quiet: The Power of Introverts in a World That Can't Stop Talking.*

Dr. Laurie Helgoe, in her book, *Introvert Power*, shares her husband's experience of dealing with her introversion and need for space. He likened it to a light being removed or a projector stopping during a feature film. I tried to keep that in mind when requesting time to myself.

I learned that introverts need space to live as their true selves. We unfold like old road maps—creases released and possibilities endless—when immersed in open-ended time. Extroverts need hits of attention and interaction to stay energized. Different methods of rejuvenating, neither better nor worse.

I found a place to rest in the words of famous loners like Henry David Thoreau and Charles Bukowski. It had been so long since I felt that kind of belonging. Like a parent's lap or a lover's embrace, the acknowledgement that cravings for solitude were not selfish or bad enveloped me in warm acceptance. It was like sitting late at night at the kitchen table with my dearest friends.

"Now, more than ever, we need our solitude. Being alone gives us the power to regulate and adjust our lives. It can teach us fortitude and the ability to satisfy our own needs. A restorer of energy, the stillness of alone experiences provides us with much-needed rest. It brings forth our longing to explore, our curiosity about the unknown, our will to be an individual, our hopes for freedom. Alone time is fuel for life." —**Dr. Ester Buchholz**

It seemed the general belief in Western culture was that if you were not interacting in a relationship you hardly existed. Others shaped and proved our existence. They talked to us and touched us, therefore we existed.

I learned that introverts dig deep into their inner worlds to find existential confirmation. When in solitude, we are in tune with our inner voice and our personal values become clearer. There is no one to refute them. Too much external stimulation and interaction, and our inner voice is muffled.

I feel connected to others even when I am alone. I have time to miss them or wonder about their feelings. A desire grows to love and engage with them.

My wish is for solitude to be an encouraged and accepted state. Those who crave it should not be ashamed or misjudged as selfish. Many of our greatest inventions and works of art were born out of solitude. The benefits of making space for reflection are endless, but below are a few of the key ones:

- More self-awareness, a chance to hear our inner voice
- Less anxiety due to a removal of the perceived gap between what we are and what we should be
- More interpersonal understanding
- More intuitive decision-making
- Appreciation of beauty
- Creation of art
- Thoughtful actions and reactions

Like Thoreau, Bukowski, and so many other writers and artists, I found solitude to be a fertile space for curiosity and ideas to bubble up and form associations where once there were none. Creativity thrives in solitude. While running on a trail, driving by myself, or dreaming lazily in the shower, sweet memories and random facts joined to become solutions to everyday dilemmas or epiphanies to be shared in my newest endeavor, at the time, *space2live*, a blog about introverts and relationships.

SLOWING DOWN/PRESENCE

The tag line for *space2live* was: Pay attention. Reflect. Evolve. Back in the days of running errands, carpooling, and constant busy-ness, I had to fight to stay awake and not get lost in the details of doing and doing. I'd had a taste of personal and creative awareness, and I wanted to learn more. I longed to slow down.

"Willing is doing something you know already, something you have been told by somebody else; there is no new imaginative understanding in it. And presently your soul gets frightfully sterile and dry because you are so quick, snappy, and efficient about doing one thing after another that you have not time for your own ideas to come in and develop and gently shine." —**Brenda Ueland,** *If You Want to Write: A Book About Art, Independence and Spirit*

The frenetic doing of modern life drained me. All of my energy went outward toward external tasks, but I was filled up by deep concentration and a new awareness of beauty.

Writing for *space2live* subconsciously forced me to become a steadfast observer. I wanted the details of the senses to fill my writing with flavor and imagery. There was a new appreciation for nuances and ironies. In order to catch those, I had to pay attention. It's hard to quickly pay attention. Presence and awareness take time.

While on vacation in the Dominican Republic, my family and I took a tour off the grounds of the resort. While riding in our tour Jeep, we passed two Dominican women sitting in a doorway of a rusted tin shack. They were talking and smiling. They waved at us as our noisy Jeep drove by. A woman on the tour made the comment that Dominicans seem to take the time to enjoy life. Another woman quickly piped up, "Not me. I get anxious if I have too much time on my hands. My mind just doesn't stop running." It struck me as interesting that the poor Dominicans seemed to be more content than the privileged tourists. I wrote about it in a post for *space2live* using sensory detail.

Staying present eases the grip of anxiety, in that it keeps our minds from wandering to a future where negative "What if..." scenarios play out. Worrying about what has not happened yet is counterproductive and stimulates the primitive and reactive part of our brain. Presence gives us a feeling of control because there is certainty in now. We can see, feel, hear, and taste what is happening now. The future is uncertain—a guessing game.

For help staying present, I began to meditate and made a daily practice of it. I would spend ten glorious minutes sitting on my closet floor each day (a mom takes her privacy wherever she can find it), noticing my breathing and keeping my brain from thinking about what to make for dinner or if the kids' vaccines were up to date. I've never had such a calm state of presence as I did when I would meditate regularly. Scientific research backs up my findings. A 2012 study done at Stanford University found that meditation practice was associated with decreases in negative emotion and social anxiety symptom severity, and used fMRI tests to show that the brains of meditators experienced measurable increases in attention-related parietal cortex neural responses (activity the more evolved part of the brain) when implementing attention regulation of negative self-beliefs.

THOSE WHO ALLOW YOU TO BE YOU

One day, years ago, I found myself sitting in the waiting area of the music school my son attended for guitar lessons. The school's owner had come out and greeted me with a kind, gentle voice and then left. Within the quiet following his departure, I listened to musical notes drifting in from nearby classrooms. I smelled candles burning, their fragrance mixing with my slow, easy breathing. I noticed my frenetic spirit, rested. Personal ideas and dreams began to seep into my consciousness. I realized it had been a long time since I felt that at home and in tune with myself (outside of meditation and solitude). I imagined being a part of an artistic world of musicians, writers, creators. A world that seemed so magical, meaningful, and—for me—out of reach. I had never been especially musically gifted or artistic.

I considered taking lessons myself ,but I was afraid to step outside of my safe routines. How would that kind of me time affect my family? Was it selfish to consider playing guitar? I kept thinking about the lessons but was hesitant to sign up .I sent an email to the music school's owner saying as much. He responded with, "Why do you feel guilty about taking time for yourself? I feel it's the best thing in the world to fill yourself up, and then it spills onto everyone else."

I started lessons. The decision changed my life.

Over the next few years, the music school provided a sacred place for my true spirit to reveal itself. My courage grew within the safe discussions that took place during my guitar lessons. The first lesson, Mike, my teacher told me of his love of the 1970s television show, *Little House on the Prairie*. I thought that was a fairly vulnerable admission for a man. I found his honesty refreshing and inspiring. I credit Mike for making lessons more than perfect scales and pristine playing. Each lesson was about learning and exploring the world as well as music. We read books together and analyzed spirituality, relationships, writers, and creativity in between guitar playing. Mike had a calm, safe presence. We became friends. He listened without judgment if I spoke of my worries about falling short in my roles as wife and mother.

I still got nervous each time I played guitar with Mike observing me (a characteristic of those with Social Anxiety Disorder), but I also experienced deep satisfaction when we played together and I made it through a whole section (mistakes included). I was in a creative setting where it was OK to just be. I didn't have to be perfect. I could play just for the pleasure of the sound, the experience, and the companionship.

YOU DON'T HAVE TO WRITE RIGHT

Buoyed by the positive experience of guitar lessons, I looked into another artistic endeavor. A friend mentioned a literary center in my area. She said it was a hangout and teaching center for writers of all levels. I checked out the website and found the course list inviting and non-intimidating.

I chose "Intuitive Writing" as one of my first forays into the world of writing. Again, the format was loose and informal. The teacher, Roxanne, wrote the mantra "Follow your energy!" at the top of the syllabus. Roxanne (a psychoanalyst) made up the intuitive writing label with the idea that we should write without censorship, without lifting the pen from the paper, and without judgment. Our thoughts should flow from our hearts, down our arms, and onto the paper. This, plus the sharing of our writing, would be healing and inspiring. Roxanne gave us prompts such as "What I really want to say is...," and then we would write off-the-cuff for twenty minutes or so. We always had a choice regarding how much, if any, of our piece we read out loud. Roxanne's gentle nature and absolute assurance there was no wrong way to write in her class quieted our inner critics. We could be vulnerable with our words. The class experienced joy and connection, with no fear of failure.

At the end of the intuitive writing class, Roxanne invited me to join a small private writing group that served as an extension of the intuitive class. She led the private group as well. I eagerly accepted the invitation.

I remember sitting around a kitchen table with my new writing group, feeling the intoxicating freedom of mutual vulnerability. We were all in various stages of learning and healing. We were looking for a place where we could remove our *masks of false bravado*. We were looking for acceptance and permission to make mistakes. In that place I wanted to share. I couldn't stop myself from sharing what had been locked down forever.

I had moved from a world where mistakes were pointed out and "right" was better than "kind," to a space where support was palpable and stories resonated. Head nodding abounded. My spirit soared. It was easy to dream and feel grateful in that space. I wanted to spread that feeling, that spaciousness—but felt stunted in my regular world.

DESPAIR: ANOTHER CHANNEL TO SELF-AWARENESS

My day-to-day family life required all of us to have our acts together. No slipping, no falling short, no showing weakness. We were McMansion-deep in the meritocracy. I don't believe anyone in my house felt safe enough to be vulnerable. There was always someone watching and waiting to exploit our soft spots. Fear was in the ether of our home. We kept breathing it in and spewing it out. We couldn't get it out of our pores. The need to achieve and keep pace with the families in our community and socioeconomic level kept us all running, burying our true selves in the pursuit.

As author Jonathon Fields says, "Self-awareness comes with an evil twin, self-judgment, which, for many, tips into fear, censorship and self-loathing with stunning efficiency."

Even though I was thriving in personal endeavors, subconsciously and consciously, I felt inadequate as a wife and mother. I didn't love my husband enough. I didn't sacrifice for my kids enough. I wasn't a *doer* naturally. Now that I knew I was an introvert, I was extra aware I wasn't quick on my feet with answers, decisions, and action steps. I didn't have an advanced degree. I didn't have a job making money.

To make up for all of those inadequacies I tried to be my family and community's version of perfect. I went against my introverted and sensitive nature. I emulated neighbors, friends and members of our community in order to receive validation.

I was so unhappy at home. I bled energy and authenticity there.

My husband would come home from work and sit in the car, dreading entering the house and dealing with the unhappiness inside. I tensed up the second I heard the garage door go up. That meant it was time to put on my competent and confident mask. Time to act like I did not spend a miserable day dealing with child meltdowns and tedious attempts to keep the house in perfect condition. Time to do my best to appear loving toward my husband, who felt like the kingpin to my misery—the reason I had to live in high gear. I did not want to fail in my duties.

The externally generated tension that pushed me to seek relief from the doctor in the form of an antidepressant now sat squarely in my chest, reminding me of all my responsibilities and where I fell short. As I struggled to sleep each night, tightness in my chest accompanied a flashing reel of responsibilities to be handled the next day.

I was now aware of my weaknesses as well as my joys, but the weaknesses dominated my everyday living, while the moments of true satisfaction only existed when I was free from my household.

CHARACTER OVER COMPETITION

In *The Road to Character*, author David Brooks says that all the people of great character in his book, including such notables as Dwight D. Eisenhower, George Marshall, and Viktor Frankl, had one pattern in common: "They all had to go down to go up. When they were in a crucible moment, they suddenly had a greater ability to see their own nature. They had to humble themselves in self-awareness if they had any hope of rising up transformed." Brooks states that in the "valley of humility," they learned to quiet the self and only in quieting the self could they see the world clearly.

While following the recipe spelled out in the language of the competitive meritocracy, we have little self-awareness. We are asleep. While experiencing moments of quiet in solitude and nurturing relationships, self-awareness arises. We begin to wake up.

As we open our eyes, self-judgment surfaces. We see or feel like we've missed out on something grand. We've assembled all of our external roles and rewards, but feel anxious. If we choose wrong, we could be cast out of our primary social circles for violating the norms. It's not easy to know what to do when we've followed others for so long.

We've never developed the inner fortitude to be able to handle popular disapproval. As an introvert, it hurts when we wake up to realize we are not the personality type our culture admires. It stings to know this, and yet it is in this time of humility that we start our transformation. We build resiliency and self-respect.

While following the recipe for self-respect, we do not look to give ourselves a competitive edge over others. We look to be better than we used to be. We confront our weaknesses. We develop our eulogy virtues. We strive to be dependable in times of stress, and morally upstanding in times of temptation. Self-respect is earned by inner triumphs, not external ones. Inner triumphs feel like home to an introvert.

CHALLENGES OF WAKING UP

One challenge of waking up is escaping the lull of résumé virtues and other people's recipes for life. We may seem independent, but our personal worth and integrity still reside in other's value systems. We lack the vocabulary to describe and execute our inner desires and eulogy virtues. Résumé virtues are always going to be a part of our makeup. They push us to explore and build external success. The problem is that we fall asleep striving to achieve and compare ourselves to others. We don't create strong inner realms that fortify us against disapproval. If we don't consistently reflect and analyze our behavior and decisions, we are bound to make the same mistakes over and over, including (unsuccessfully) dating the same kind of people and (unhappily) working the same kind of job. Eventually, tension and anxiety tell some of us we are missing out on personal growth, significance, and meaning.

Tension, solitude, paying attention, and positive relationships wake us up.

Action steps for waking up:

1. Notice the places where you feel a tension or dissonance in your life. Do you tense up when a significant person in your life enters the room? Does Sunday night bring about a feeling of dread because you have to go to work the next morning? Are you tired of spending every Friday night at home watching TV? Does it sound intriguing to get out and meet a few more people?

2. Engage in and protect your solitude. See time alone as vital to your well-being, just like sleep or exercise. Explain to your children and partners that solitude is self-preservation for you, not rejection of them.

3. While in solitude or in a group, use a prompt such as "The last time I was really angry..." to start ten to twenty minutes of uncensored writing. Do not stop writing the whole time. Do not edit. Let the subconscious become conscious. Share with others if you feel comfortable.

4. Pay attention. At night as you lie in bed, picture a scene from the day and describe it in writing or in your head, including details from all five senses.

5. Notice where you feel energized or at home. Who, if anyone, is with you? List your relationships that feel most nurturing and nonjudgmental. Spend more time with them. Try new things with these safe people. People we love and admire positively influence our behavior and character.

Another challenge of waking up or self-awareness is the self-judgment that comes along with it. Once we are aware of our traits and flaws, we realize others are aware of them too. While in this "valley of humility," our ego quiets. We focus on victories over our weaknesses rather than on victories over others. In confronting our shortcomings, we build self-respect.

Action steps for ameliorating self-judgment:

1. Foster self-respect. Put yourself in a humbling situation like taking guitar lessons without any prior experience or skill. Let yourself make mistakes and survive.

2. On your day off, instead of watching Netflix all day, offer to help someone and come through for them.

3. Collaborate with someone you generally compete with at school or work.

Practice Two: Calming Our Nervous System Principles of Self-Care

The timing for writing this chapter on self-care was perfect. I was having one of those weeks where all of my energy flowed outward and very little flowed back toward me. My closest relationships required a lot of assistance and attention, but were unable to offer the same in return. I helped a friend move. Dealt with relationship challenges from my teenage son. Experienced no emotional intimacy with my significant other. Ran a million errands. Managed several house repairs. Slept poorly and managed to contract a rash on my face. Needless to say, my emotions ran high and my energy tank was running on empty.

I'd been in this low place before. Self-awareness and experience provided guidance.

I continually asked myself, "What would fill me up? What do I need to recover from this downward spiral?"

Here is the short list of answers:

- Positive emotional connection with others

- Time to myself

- Creativity, insight and meaningful work

- Exercise

- Sleep

APPLY SELF-AWARENESS

Before starting on the list, it is important to note that self-soothing requires knowing ourselves well, which is accomplished by using the self-awareness tools we discussed in the previous chapter:

- Notice where tension exists and where it doesn't

- Pay attention and stay in the present

- Experiment within your most emotionally safe relationships to determine your skills and weaknesses

- Slow down and under-schedule yourself to hear your inner voice

It is vital to know our likes and dislikes and how-to re-center ourselves. By knowing ourselves, we take care of ourselves and have answers when others inquire or test our boundaries.

Once we have self-awareness, it is easier to administer self-care. In fact, as I wrote this chapter I noticed a lot of overlap between the subject matter in "Practice One: Waking Up" and this chapter on calming our nervous system with self-care. I found it difficult at times to decide which chapter to place certain information in. Solitude, for example, is mentioned under both practices. It seems that as we learn about ourselves we nurture ourselves, and vice versa.

POSITIVE EMOTIONAL EXPRESSION

Although our culture often undervalues emotions and overvalues intellect, emotions came first in our brain's evolutionary development. According to neuroscientists, we felt emotions millions of years before we generated thoughts. So rather than being thinking creatures that feel, we are actually feeling creatures that think. Some emotions seem like something we should hide. If others see us as emotional, we feel weak or not as together. If we show our feelings, we appear out of control.

But emotions serve a purpose. They warn us of danger, by putting us on alert and making us pay attention with fight or flight responses. Our emotions are our body's way of communicating with us. They talk to us and allow us to create deeper connections with ourselves by helping us see what truly matters. Emotions, if shared openly and validated, also help us connect with others and keep us from feeling alone.

If we internalize and suppress our feelings for too long, it can wreak havoc on our physical and mental health. Some common side effects of suppressed emotions are:

- Depression

- Low energy

- Eating, sleeping and learning problems

- Digestive issues, muscle tension, headaches or back pain

- Irritability

- Anxiety

- Feeling alone

- Wondering if we matter

- Shallow relationships

Leaving our emotions undifferentiated and unexpressed causes a downward spiral, like the one I was in when I started composing this chapter.

The first step to combating emotional decline is to name or put words to what we feel. Scientific evidence shows labeling emotions with specific words provides relief. A study done in 2007 by Dr. Matthew Lieberman, Director of Social Cognitive Neuroscience Laboratory at the University of California, Los Angeles, Dr. Naomi Eisenberger, Director of Social and Affective Neuroscience Laboratory at the University of California, Los Angeles, and their colleagues had participants look at pictures of people with emotional facial expressions. Using fMRI technology, the scientists were able to see the amygdala and other limbic sections of the brain light up with activity in reaction to the pictures. When asked to name the emotions seen, the activity in the amygdala diminished and activity in the prefrontal cortex increased. Labeling the emotions moved the reaction from the primitive and more alarm-setting region of the brain (amygdala, limbic system) to the more evolved, more decisive and in-control region (prefrontal cortex), thus leading to a calmer feeling.

When working with clients, I have an exercise I use to check in with them regarding their current emotional state. The tool is also helpful for them to use on their own, when they want to re-center themselves. The acronym I created for the exercise is N.A.A.P.T.T. and it stands for:

N: Name emotions
A: Accept emotions
A: Attribute emotions
P: Positive relational memory
T: Talk to others
T: Take action

I remember the acronym by thinking N, double A, P, double T or if read phonetically it sounds like *napped*. Naps provide relief.

N for naming emotions. This is a direct use of the Lieberman study results. Naming what we feel shifts how our brains process the emotions. Using specific words to articulate feelings alleviates stress. It causes us to feel more in control and therefore more at ease.

A for accepting emotions. As mentioned, many times we feel bad for having emotions. We think we should be composed and strong all the time. The truth is that emotions provide feedback, which is valuable to our decision-making. We need to listen to the feelings and allow them to guide us. Another good point to remember is that emotions pass. Like clouds in the sky or the daily weather, they move on after a time. Resisting them only gives them power over us, as shown in the list of results from suppressed feelings.

A for attributing emotions. This is the step where I ask clients what has changed recently and why they may be feeling this way. Have they experienced this feeling before and, if so, what was the cause at that time? Many of our feelings stem from past experiences, especially those encountered during childhood. Figuring out and stating the narrative from our past helps soothe old wounds. We'll talk more about this in Practice Five.

P for positive relational memory or PRM. Psychiatrist and expert in relational psychopharmacology Amy Banks defines PRMs as a time you remember feeling safe and happy in another person's presence. I advise clients to keep a mental or written list of these moments. I use photos on my phone or a list I created in a notes application to remind me of such times. Focusing on these memories increases dopamine in our brain, which creates a feeling of pleasure.

The final two Ts are the action steps. They go beyond reflection. The action steps are where the hardest but most valuable personal growth occurs.

T for talk to others. Now for introverts and those with social anxiety, this may seem more daunting than helpful. I am not suggesting you find a social gathering and spill your guts. I suggest thinking about the relationships that offer the most emotional safety and reach out to them. This may be one person or it may even be a pet. The important thing is to express your feelings. Allow your emotions to connect you with another being.

T for take action. For some situations, taking action could mean talking to someone; either your closest companions or the person you feel is the origin of the emotion. This may mean saying no to a request of your time or standing up to a power-hungry coworker. Other examples of action taking are working on a fitness plan or moving to a new city.

DECIDE TO TAKE ACTION

A favorite personal mantra is "Action dissolves fear." I know stewing in my own pity and frustration does no good. I have to stop the ruminating. I have to do something.

Before we take action, we make decisions. Decisions stop the loop of worry, which indecision exacerbates.

I've learned from experience that I may not make the perfect choice right off the bat. Often there are too many choices, and the fallout is unpredictable. I use self-awareness and a keen knowledge of my preferences to make the best (although not perfect) decision.

Neuroscience backs up the benefits of making a good-enough decision. In *The Upward Spiral*, author and neuroscientist Dr. Alex Korb states that recognizing that good enough is good enough activates the dorsolateral prefrontal cortex part of the brain, which helps us feel more in control. Dr. Korb also says creating intentions and setting goals engages the prefrontal cortex of the brain in a positive way, reducing worry and anxiety. Making decisions also helps us overcome activity in the brain's striatum. The striatum often pulls us toward negative impulses and routines. Lastly, decisions help us find solutions to our problems, which calms our limbic system (emotional feeling part of the brain) and allows us to act instead of stew.

THE POWER OF INTERACTING

I craved emotional connection. I wanted to have meaningful conversations. I wanted to feel heard, understood, and loved. Life had been busy lately; there was no time for such quality interactions.

The need to interact poses a conundrum for the introvert. As seen in my list of how to recover from my downward spiral, I wanted time to myself as well as intimate connection. Introverts want connection, but recharge in solitude or with a select few people. Interacting may be more effortful for us, but the results are worth it.

Scientific studies demonstrate humans do not thrive when alone. Our species' evolution and mental wiring dictate we be social. Studies show being socially rejected activates the same parts of your brain as physical pain does. Often if our mood starts to decline, it means we need to be with others. A sense of belonging and a need to be needed are two powerful drivers for humans. Just being in a populated environment without actually interacting helps elevate our mood. Pets count as options for interaction, which should put some introverts' minds to rest.

BRING ON THE OXYTOCIN

Carrying on nonjudgmental conversations with others builds trust and attachment, which kick-starts an upward spiral of emotions with a release of the hormone *oxytocin*.[2] Oxytocin is produced:

- During sex

- With soft touching

- When we feel someone trusts us

- When we feel we can trust others

Oxytocin decreases the feelings of stress, fear and pain. It is sometimes called the cuddle drug or love hormone.

During one study, oxytocin showed an antidepressant effect in mice that had minor injuries but were paired with another mouse postinjury. Having a partner during recovery increased the amount of oxytocin in the mice's systems. Mice with injuries and no partners developed symptoms of depression and gave up easily on difficult tasks. The paired mice showed less depression and more resilience.

Stress and anxiety are caused by reactions in the limbic system— the part of your brain responsible for emotions and the forming of memories. The amygdala, hypothalamus, and hippocampus are all part of the limbic system. Oxytocin quiets an overreactive amygdala and increases communication between the amygdala and prefrontal cortex, which helps regulate our emotions. It also stimulates the area of the brain where the pleasure chemical dopamine is produced.

HOW TO INCREASE YOUR BODY'S OXYTOCIN PRODUCTION

Various forms of touching: massages, long hugs, orgasms, handshakes, and petting animals all enhance oxytocin production. Trusting, being trusted, and feeling safe emotionally with another person also release oxytocin.

Some of us did not have the best relationships with our parents growing up. Unfortunately, oxytocin enhances our feelings about close relationships based on our relationships with our parents. If our relationship with our parents was difficult, we will have a tendency to react negatively to close relationships. This can be improved though rebuilding positive neural circuits and increasing oxytocin production. So, there is hope! Positive and secure relationships build new circuits.

Another positive way relationships affect our lives is by sharing eye contact. Couple therapist Dr. Stan Tatkin says eye gazing relaxes us and makes us feel connected because it turns off the hypervigilant search for threats of the limbic system (you've already let the person in close enough to look into their eyes) and turns on the trusting, fully engaged, more evolved prefrontal cortex.

TIME ALONE

The opposite of seeking interaction is seeking time alone. Despite all of the benefits of connecting with others, this introvert still needs time alone.

Perhaps it is, as Marti Olsen Laney says in *The Introvert Advantage*, that my innate introverted nature is more sensitive to stimulation and uses longer neural pathways and more parts of my brain to process incoming information. This would definitely explain a deep desire to get away from too much stimulation. My brain needs a break.

Or perhaps the insecure attachment style I developed as a child causes me to seek autonomy and avoid rejection. The lack of consistent availability of my parents encouraged self-reliance and self-soothing. Because of the unavailability of emotional support, I adopted an avoidant attachment style which causes me to withdraw to self-regulate when the going gets tough. We will talk about attachment styles and their effects more in Practice Five.

SPIRITUALITY ON MY OWN

Either way, I need quiet time to myself. Solitude provides space to develop self-awareness as was mentioned in Practice One. Simply listening to music, reading, or meditating renews me. In solitude, I rest. I daydream about and long for my important relationships. I hear my inner voice and listen for hints to what I truly value. In this way, solitude provides a spiritual experience. It puts me in touch with my truths and the truths of humanity. It directs me and renews my commitment to do and be better than I was yesterday. Be a better mother, daughter, partner, friend, writer, personal coach, and human. I get the calming effect of touching my spiritual core without attending a formal religious ceremony. Formal religions and rituals may have their place for us too, but it is important to note that we do not have to participate with others in order to experience spiritual grace.

Alone I do not have to reconcile what I know in my thoughts with what is going on in the external world. I don't have to be perfect. Any social anxiety I have dims in solitude. I can concentrate and perform the delicate process of recognizing patterns and making associations, which often leads to creativity.

CREATIVITY, INSIGHT AND MEANINGFUL WORK

"The creative person is constantly seeking to discover himself, to remodel his own identity, and to find meaning in the universe by means of what he creates. He finds this to be a valuable integrating process which, like meditation or prayer, has little to do with other people, but which has its own separate validity. His most significant moments are those in which he attains some new insight, or makes some new discovery; and these moments are chiefly, if not invariably, those in which he is alone." —Anthony Storr, *Solitude: A Return to the Self*

Composing this chapter, and this entire book for that matter, served as an exercise in discovering new facets of myself, finding meaning in my work, and gaining insight about introversion, anxiety and relationships.

LONG-TERM GOALS CREATE MEANING

According to Dr. Korb in *The Upward Spiral*, people are at their best when moving toward a long-term meaningful goal. Dopamine (pleasure and motivation neurotransmitter and chemical messenger) is produced in the body when the goal is achieved and with each step we make toward the goal. Having a long-term plan also allows our prefrontal cortex (highly developed part of our brain that gives us a sense of control) to effectively organize our actions. Ill-defined goals do not lead to the same level of satisfaction or the same level of activity in the brain because the brain is unable to determine when a goal is achieved. Creating specific, meaningful and achievable long-term goals can even reverse the effects of depression.

Tapping into creativity is also an excellent way to boost our mood. Creativity with a long-term end goal is even better.

FINDING CREATIVITY IN IDLENESS

Creativity fascinates me because it is both a process of persistence and craftsmanship and a process of sitting back and allowing random ideas to mingle and copulate. It is often in moments of idleness that our purest and most revelatory insights and creations develop. As we drive down empty highways, take long hot showers, go for long but lazy walks and sit daydreaming in a room bathed in sunshine, we expand. We come up with new solutions to our problems, new material for our book, new ways to communicate with loved ones, new chords to a song, etc.

> *"But if it is the dreamy idleness that children have, an idleness when you walk alone for a long, long time, or take a long, dreamy time at dressing, or lie in bed at night and thoughts come and go, or dig in a garden, or drive a car for many hours alone, or play the piano, or sew, or paint ALONE; or an idleness...*
> *With all my heart, I tell you and reassure you: at such times, you are being slowly filled and recharged with warm imagination, with wonderful, living thoughts."* —**Brenda Ueland,** *If You Want to Write: A Book About Art,*
> **Independence and Spirit**

FINDING CREATIVITY IN ACTION

Sir Ken Robinson, noted British public speaker and expert on education, creativity, and innovation, describes creativity as applied imagination. He believes our capacity for creativity allows us to rethink our lives and find our way to what drives us. He says we cannot just sit around thinking about creativity. It requires acting on it, doing something.

If I would have only sat and thought about writing this chapter, it would not have had the same mood-boosting effect as actually stringing sentences together, typing them on the computer, and sharing them with you. The structure and some of the components of this chapter were contrived while showering, so idleness played a part in my creative process, just as the quote above from Brenda Ueland says, and so does taking action as Sir Ken Robinson says, because after coming up with ideas in the shower, I typed them on my laptop.

As mentioned in the action steps for "Practice One: Waking Up", it is a good idea to ask ourselves where we feel most energized and where we feel most at home. The answers to these questions serve as signposts to our creativity and meaningful work.

ARE YOU IN YOUR ELEMENT?

In his book, *The Element: How Finding Your Passion Changes Everything*, Sir Ken Robinson describes a state of being he calls *the element* as the meeting point between natural aptitude and personal passion. This is the ultimate state for growth and learning. In their element, people connect with something fundamental to their sense of identity, purpose and well-being. People often describe finding their element as an epiphany. It's a sense of defining whom they really are and what they are meant to do with their lives. The element has two main features and two conditions for being in it. The two features are aptitude and passion. The conditions are attitude and opportunity.

An aptitude is a natural gift for doing something. It's an intuitive understanding of how it works and how to use it. Finding and developing our strengths is part of becoming who we really are. Sir Ken Robinson says, "We don't know who we can be until we know what we can do."

An important note is that just because we have an aptitude for something does not mean we have a passion for it. My middle son has an incredible head for math, but he does not enjoy doing it. Being in our element means taking a deep pleasure in what we do.

Attitude is our personal perspective on our circumstances and ourselves. Our basic character, our sense of self-worth, the perceptions and expectations of those around us, all influence our attitude. Our perception of our circumstances depends largely on what we expect of ourselves.

If we do not encounter the right opportunities we may never know our aptitudes. It's hard to know you are an excellent surfer if you live in the middle of a desert. A lot depends on the opportunities we have, the ones we create and if we take advantage of them.

Often finding people with similar passions leads us to our element. We have to explore different opportunities to find like-minded people. Other people often point out our skills or aptitudes too, as we do theirs.

HOW DO WE KNOW WHEN WE ARE IN OUR ELEMENT?

First of all, it is possible to come to our element in a myriad of ways. Some people find it through intense physical activity, taking risks, competition, or a sense of danger. For others, including many introverts, the element may come through more passive activities such as gardening, meditation, intense contemplation, painting, or writing.

One of the strongest signs of being in our element is a sense of doing what we are meant to do. There is a freedom and a feeling of authenticity. Ideas flow through us. Time feels different in our element, or as some people (including athletes) call it, *the zone*. Time moves quickly and fluidly when we are doing what we are good at and love.

THE ELEMENT AND FLOW

Some of you may be thinking the element sounds a lot like psychologist Mihaly Csikszentmihalyi's (phonetically chicks-sent-me-HIGH-ee) concept of *flow*. Dr. Csikszentmihalyi describes flow as joy, creativity, and the process of total involvement with life. The components of flow create an optimal experience. The components include: facing a challenge that requires a skill we possess; complete absorption in an activity; clear goals and feedback; deep concentration that allows us to forget everything else; the loss of self-consciousness; and the sense that time transforms. The key component in flow is that it is an end in itself. The activity consumes us and becomes intrinsically rewarding.

Both being in our element and being in flow give us energy. The experience does not drain us, even if it is physically or mentally taxing. This kind of energy can be a big boost to an introvert's well-being. Instead of overstimulating us, it recharges us, often in a productive and rewarding way.

FLOW STATES MAKE LIFE WORTH LIVING

I've had a fascination with the delicious, dreamy, creative flow state since I was a child. I believe the steady presence of flow experiences in my life is the reason for my overall contentedness and satisfaction. Jamie Wheal of *The Flow Genome Project* says flow is the source code for intrinsic motivation. In my opinion, intrinsic motivation and curiosity keep life engaging and interesting and therefore fulfilling.

Mihaly Csikszentmihalyi, mentioned earlier, is known as the father of flow theory. Noting that levels of happiness did not increase with increased personal income, he set out to find out what does bring happiness and satisfaction. Interviewing creative individuals such as scientists and artists, he found many of them frequently experienced feelings of losing themselves, timelessness, effortlessness, and ecstasy. During those periods they felt they were outside of everyday experiences. Time and movement felt fluid. Certain activities brought about a sense of flow.

"Being completely involved in an activity for its own sake. The ego falls away. Time flies. Every action, movement, and thought follows inevitably from the previous one, like playing jazz. Your whole being is involved, and you're using your skills to the utmost." —**Mihaly Csikszentmihalyi, describing "flow"**

DO INTROVERTS EXPERIENCE FLOW DIFFERENTLY DUE TO STIMULATION SENSITIVITY?

Flow states, like Abraham Maslow's peak experiences, do not happen continuously. Behind the flow feeling is a cascade of brain chemicals produced by the right mix of challenge and skill in our activities. There is a cycle to flow which requires us to go through different phases such as struggle and recovery. We all have different triggers that prompt us to enter the flow cycle.

As a sensitive introvert, my go-to triggers for flow are mental. I get the feeling of timelessness and spontaneous creativity via deep thinking and solitary, soothing, and reflective pursuits. Low stimulation is important. Others may access flow in more adrenaline-fueled, highly stimulating activities, but times of stillness and repetitive activity allow my mind to wander in a creatively productive and fulfilling way. Reading, writing, meditation, and meaningful conversations often set my nervous system at ease and allow flow to enter. This state of mind is addictive and has me seeking quiet time to get the restorative feeling again.

WHAT IS THE ENEMY OF MY FLOW STATE?

Interruptions and distractions are the enemy of flow state. As a young woman in my twenties, I worked as an office manager for a small IT recruiting firm in Chicago. I used to love to do repetitive data entry / accounting work. It allowed my mind to meander through meaningful memories or dally through dinner plans. When my boss entered the office each day, bursting through the door, taking huge strides down the center aisle, delegating work as she walked, my mindless work and yummy reflective trance were disrupted like a rock thrown into a tranquil pond.

Now as a fortysomething trying to work from home, the potential for interruptions is the same. My phone, my children, and my own distracted mind pull me away from the contemplative scene necessary for full creative productivity. Writing is the perfect blend of challenge and skill for me. If left alone in stillness, I can create sentences I'm proud of. I can slip into the beautiful place where my inner critic is silent and ideas flow.

FLOW NOT LIMITED TO SOLITARY MENTAL PURSUITS

Achieving the flow state is not limited to solitary pursuits for me, although they are the most reliable triggers. I also find myself in an otherworldly state while working with my coaching clients, talking with close friends/family or while making love. Again, there is a prerequisite of calm necessary to bring on the flow feeling. Intuitively guiding my clients and fostering their potential is hugely satisfying. It's just the right blend of challenge and skill to put me in the zone. Conversing with my friends and family about intimate, expansive topics like personal growth and relationships brings on the good, fulfilling state of fluidity too.

Not only is flow achievable through social versus solitary endeavors, it can also be induced by physical triggers versus mental ones. In the past, dancing was the only physical activity that brought about the flow feeling. Music is a key reason for that. Music taps into rich brain chemicals for me.

Now, I occasionally have epiphanies, heightened creativity, and moments of effortlessness while running. This is what many call a "runner's high" or "being in the zone."

I also find intensely focusing on the physical sensations and emotional connection during sex opens up the door to the dreamlike, oxytocin and dopamine-laden experience of flow.

In both running and making love I am sufficiently challenged, engaged, and motivated, which makes them fulfilling, life-enriching endeavors. Which makes me want to do them again.

When I took the *Flow Fundamentals Course* through *The Flow Genome Project*, I learned one of the key steps to reaching flow state is securing our physical health. Our mind, body, and spirit are not able to reach optimal performance if they are deficient in quality sleep, food or fitness. We all know how distracting and delaying a minor bout of sickness can be. A cold or the flu can narrow our focus to getting well. One bad night of sleep can affect us for days. If we want to live offensively versus defensively, we have to be in tip-top condition.

EXERCISE

Exercise is one of the most straightforward and effective ways to change our overall well-being. Moving and challenging our body produces and reduces the same neurochemicals that most antidepressants target.

Changing our body and mindset from sedentary to active requires making a decision, taking a step (however small) toward fitness and sticking with it. Our old friend, decision-making, again is the kick-starter to an upward spiral. If you'll recall, making a decision (a good-enough decision), starts a cascade of positive activity in the brain. This activity helps us organize our actions, pull away from negative routines, and ultimately calm our nervous system.

I know how easy it is to embrace inertia. The couch, the television, our beds, the to-do list, our friends, and family all vie for our attention and time. It's so easy to put exercise off, but again, fitness and the next topic, sleep, are the two most straightforward and powerful paths to feeling incredible. If we make improvements in these two areas alone, a positive shift will occur that affects every other area of our lives.

As I mentioned earlier, self-awareness and self-care are closely related. Before I took the leap and signed up for guitar lessons, I made a decision to invest in my physical health. My then husband and I joined the local health club. It was a beautiful modern facility with childcare for the kids. I needed a focus other than our children. Subconsciously, perhaps I was striving to figure out what I was made of. What could I handle physically and mentally?

My husband and I had always been health-conscious. We knew intellectually that taking care of our bodies was important but this time we dove deeper and made it more personal. We each signed up to work one-on-one with trainers. I know not everyone is able to afford a personal trainer. It is truly a luxury. For me, it was one of the best decisions I ever made and well worth the money. It forced accountability and commitment. My trainer challenged the hell out of me and I needed that. The original intention was to work with him for a month, learn what exercises to do, and then work independently. I ended up training with Michael for three years. We did not work together one-on-one the whole time. The last two years were in a group setting, which was more cost-effective.

The biggest bonus from the intense fitness training I did with Michael was an uptick in my self-confidence. Not just because I looked better, but because I felt better and I accomplished my fitness goals. I worked through the arduous process of improving my fitness and succeeded. I proved to myself I could stick with something difficult and reap the results.

One of my proudest and most satisfying moments was when I was talking with Michael one day about my sister. He asked if she was an athlete like me. My sister was definitely an athlete. She'd played volleyball, basketball and softball all through high school and into college. The magical point to his comment was that he thought I was an athlete too. No one had ever called me an athlete. This man in peak physical condition with a master's degree in physiology thought I was athletic. I think I stood a couple inches taller after that session.

As beneficial as personal training was for me, it is absolutely not necessary for physical health. We can find yoga classes on YouTube, play ball with our kids in the driveway or take the dog for a walk. The crucial thing is to move our bodies consistently. Have compassion for ourselves when we mess up and do not hit the gym or make time for exercise. Do not give up! Do not berate yourself! Start again the next day. The amount of tries we get to do fitness right is limitless.

According to the neuroscientist Dr. Korb, exercise is like steroids for our brains. It causes an increase in nerve growth factors, which make our brain stronger and more resilient. One interesting fact is that voluntarily choosing to exercise creates more neuron development than being forced to, although both stimulate neuron growth.

Studies also show that exercise increases serotonin activity. Serotonin is a neurotransmitter found primarily in our intestines but also in our brains that helps with motivation and mood elevation. It has many purposes such as bowel function and letting us know when our appetite is sated, but for our discussion we will focus on the mood-elevating properties. Body movement increases the firing rate of serotonin neurons, which causes them to release more serotonin. We do not have to do formal exercise to get the serotonin to flow. Yard work, house cleaning, or walking around a mall all stimulate serotonin production. Serotonin gives us a feeling of calm and helps us achieve more restorative sleep.

Along with serotonin, endorphins, dopamine, and norepinephrine all increase with exercise. Endorphins are what give us that "runner's high." They decrease pain and anxiety. Dopamine affects pleasure, focus, and decision-making. Norepinephrine helps us concentrate. It, like serotonin, is one of the chemicals mimicked in antidepressants. Another big benefit of exercise is that it reduces stress hormones like cortisol and adrenaline.

Fitness and an active lifestyle provide the natural drugs we need to keep our mood lifted. I am sure you have all heard this before. I know the feeling of not wanting to be active. I want you to know the exhilarating feeling of completing your workout. Dopamine is released when we finish. Just planning to work out shifts our thinking from our lazy habit-entrenched neural pathways to the prefrontal "take charge" region of our brain.

Lastly, exercise promotes nourishing sleep. If we exercise during the day we will experience increased slow-wave sleep (more restorative) and reduced REM sleep (an active stage of sleep) at night. More about this in the next section.

Starting a new workout routine feels draining at first, but eventually we notice more energy and vitality throughout the day. Ordinarily arduous tasks feel easier. It's less effortful to run around with our kids.

I distinctly remember throwing a ball around with my sons in the yard one day and liking it. This was new. To be honest, in the past I was less than enthusiastic about such endeavors. I am more of an *indoorsy* type, but my increased fitness level made my mind and body more interested, willing, and capable of participating.

Stephen Covey of *The 7 Habits of Highly Effective People* says that by exercising we develop muscles of proactivity. Those proactive muscles cause us to act based on the value of physical well-being rather than reacting to all of the forces that keep us from exercising. In doing so, we profoundly affect our self-esteem, our self-confidence and our self-discipline.

Take that first step to get the cycle started. Here is a list of possible first steps to get you moving:

- Put exercise on your calendar

- Put on your workout clothes and shoes

- Join a fitness club or class

- Plan to meet a friend for a workout

- Do sit ups or pushups during commercial breaks (don't fast-forward through the commercials, let them be a workout space)

- Buy a new water bottle or workout shirt

- Search for fitness routines online

SLEEP

Sleep is the last, but definitely not least, subject I want to discuss that helps calm our nervous system. Poor sleep is one of the biggest contributors to developing depression and staying depressed. Both quantity and quality of sleep affect our life satisfaction.

In *The Upward Spiral*, Dr. Korb states that mentally poor sleep worsens our mood, lowers our pain threshold and interferes with learning and memory. It deters our focus and makes us more impulsive. Lack of good sleep also affects us physically. It can increase blood pressure, elevate stress levels and harm the immune system. Studies show poor sleep leads to poor eating choices and weight gain as well. It can even lead to an increased risk of drug or alcohol addiction.

Years ago, while training for a volunteer position with the juvenile justice system, I attended a seminar on chemical dependency. The director of a well-respected rehabilitation center spoke to our group. She said, "Lack of sleep is crazy-making." She'd seen the effects of poor sleep in many of the chemically dependent patients in her center. People think a drink before bed will relax them and help them sleep but in reality it affects their sleep stage progression (architecture) and the more often alcohol is used to ease into sleep the less it works. Alcohol abuse and depression both can lead to reductions in the amount of slow wave sleep and increases in the amount of REM sleep we experience, thus lowering the quality of sleep overall.

Sleep is comprised of several stages from stage one where we first drift off into a light sleep to the final stage, REM (rapid eye movement) sleep, where our brain's electrical activity is high. The most restorative sleep takes place in stages three and four when the electrical activity slows dramatically. This is called slow-wave sleep.

If we are woken up during the cycle the proper progression is disrupted and we automatically start the process over again at stage one, possibly missing the renewing sleep of stages three and four. This is one reason why it is crucial to strive for uninterrupted sleep.

We all have daily chemical fluctuations in our bodies that help monitor our hunger, body temperature and alertness. These fluctuations are called circadian rhythms. They tell our bodies when to prepare for sleep and waking up. Circadian rhythms also affect hormones like cortisol, testosterone and melatonin. Both cortisol and melatonin affect sleep.

Circadian rhythms are synchronized to daytime by exposure to the sun or bright lights. Unnatural lights from lamps, televisions, phones, computers, etc. mess with our circadian rhythms. It is best to align our bedtime and wake time with our natural rhythms, which does not mean we have to go to bed when the sun goes down and wake up when the sun comes up. It simply means to start preparing for sleep after the sun goes down. Turn off unnecessary lights, reduce screen time and stick to a consistent bedtime as much as possible (even on weekends). During the day spend some time in the sun. This will keep the rhythms running efficiently and also boost serotonin production.

I often go to bed at the same time but wake up around three or four in the morning with my mind going 100 MPH. This kind of waking is usually caused by stress or an overly busy mind, which makes for increased activity in my brain during what are supposed to be the restorative stages of slow wave sleep.

I've learned to use reading as a solution for this disruption of my sleep cycle. I do not read anything too stimulating. Fiction I find entertaining rather than educational works best. Tolstoy's Anna Karenina is a perfect calming read, for example.

Another trick I've learned is prior to going to sleep, to write down the things I'm worried about or contemplating. If I forget to do this before going to sleep it still helps if I do it when I wake up at three or four.

Change in room temperature, hunger, the secretion of stress hormones (cortisol) and bright lights suddenly shown in the room, can also cause premature waking. Make sure your room is comfortable, you have a quality snack before bed (not simple carbohydrates, they get processed quickly leaving the body hungry again) and stress is kept to a minimum.

Some guidelines for excellent sleep are:

- Sleep in a continuous block. Most people need around eight hours. Don't try to fool yourself thinking you only need four hours. Side note: Naps are not suggested because they affect optimal sleep at night.

- Keep your bedroom for sleeping and sex only. When you walk into your room at night, your body will start the process of preparing for bed, including creating melatonin, which is a hormone derived from serotonin that prepares you for sleep.

- Have a bedtime routine. This may include anything from brushing your teeth to doing yoga to reading. The important thing is to keep it consistent and calm.

- Avoid caffeine or alcohol. Even if you can fall asleep caffeinated, it will disrupt your sleep stage progression and cause diminished renewal. The same with alcohol.

- Don't eat a large meal just before bed. Don't drink a lot before bed either. Digestion can disrupt sleep, as can many trips to the bathroom.

- Exercise! It boosts serotonin (which breaks down into melatonin) and sets us up for more slow-wave sleep.

The more serotonin produced in the body, the more slow-wave sleep we experience and the less REM sleep. As mentioned earlier serotonin production increases with exercise and exposure to light.

Sleep alleviates pain as well. Our pain thresholds lower if sleep is disrupted. Once again, continuous sleep is crucial. Without it, we experience pain as worse than it is. If we sleep well, our brains release endorphins that act as painkillers. Intense exercise also releases endorphins.

Sleep and stress levels are intrinsically linked. Although, it may not be possible to remove stress from our lives, we do have some control over our sleep patterns. If we improve our sleep, we can reduce our stress.

GETTING OUT OF A DOWNWARD SPIRAL

What did I do to get out of my funk? I told my partner I felt emotional and distracted. He responded quickly by asking what was going on, demonstrating I could count on him, thus increasing my level of trust. I also benefited from the caresses and hugs he gave me later.

I attended a church service where I felt a sense of belonging and had my values validated, again increasing my trust, easing off on the limbic reaction, and creating oxytocin.

I decided to reserve half of the weekend for solitude and writing. I told my family and partner of my intention and allowed myself to get into thirteen hours of uninterrupted, delicious, creative flow state. I was in my element. I was productive and passionate. I felt a deep sense of satisfaction by the end of the day.

I participated in a dance class complete with positive socializing, upbeat music, excellent cardio and strength enhancing exercise and supportive affirmations from the instructor. I left the class feeling sexy, confident, and energized.

I went to bed around 11 o'clock and slept for a solid seven-plus hours. It was glorious. Sleep also has the added benefit of improving our appearance. Fewer bags under the eyes and more supple skin come with excellent sleep.

Everything I did filled me up and led to reduced stress. I felt rejuvenated and ready to give to the world.

Administering self-care is not easy. There are many challenges. We feel selfish taking the time. We do not have time to fit it in. We may already be in fight-or-flight mode and our brains are hijacked with stress hormones. We don't have enough supportive relationships to encourage our self-care.

Once again Stephen Covey had it right when he said, "This is the single most powerful investment we can ever make in life—investment in ourselves, in the only instrument we have with which to deal with life and to contribute."

CHALLENGES TO CALMING OUR NERVOUS SYSTEM

We often feel selfish about taking care of ourselves. We feel there is just plain no time to fit it in.

Yes, there is.

We must take action to administer self-care. Here are action steps recommended for introverts or anyone who feels drained:

1. If there is something on your calendar that is not essential to you or your family's mental or physical health, it is dispensable. Stop saying yes to activities that do not serve you or your family. Are the activities empty calories like a cupcake with sprinkles or do they nourish you? If it makes you feel empty, remove it from your schedule and insert an endeavor that lights you up.

2. When feeling upset or anxious run through the steps of N.A.A.P.T.T. Name the emotions you feel. Accept them. Attribute them to something. Recall a positive relational memory. Talk with someone and take action.

3. Set aside quiet time to consider where your passion and talent intersect. Where do you lose track of time? Where does your inner critic quiet?

4. Make a decision and plan to do the thing or go to the place where your answer to number three exists.

5. Move your body. Take one step toward physical activity.

6. Protect your sleep. Practice going to sleep at the same time and waking up at the same time for a week. Darken and quiet your bedroom. Establish a bedtime routine.

Practice Three: Becoming Whole Principles of Self-Esteem, Self-Expression and Self-Discipline

I live to get lost in books, websites, podcasts and research about personal development, relationships and optimal psychology.

I recall, as a child, my classmates complaining about having to sit through a lecture in school. For me, nothing seemed better. To this day, I still love lectures, listening and sitting. I move into the deep thinker's flow state when I read, do research and learn new things. My inner critic shuts up. Time distorts in such a way that four hours feel like one. Ideas and epiphanies sprout out of rich fertile mind loam. The pursuit of self-awareness and personal development comes naturally to me. I can't really explain it and I can't stop doing it.

Why did I share that with you? Because I'm an expert at *being*. I can meditate, empathize, process, ponder, be still, absorb, pray, learn, observe, visualize, and wonder with the best of them! However, I am only average at taking action. I am only satisfactory at pulling it all together and making it useful.

I've learned I'm not alone. Quite a few people have trouble turning their knowledge and thoughts into concrete applications. They simply get by in an unconscious cloud of doing the bare minimum and *shoulds*. As I learned from relationship coach and creator of *The Smart Couple Podcast* Jayson Gaddis, *shoulds* are for those not willing to put in the effort to know themselves or those incapable of rejecting social norms. In other words, if we don't expand our self-awareness and subsequently challenge ourselves to act on our authenticity, even if it means going against the social grain, we remain stuck in a thinking quicksand. We don't move forward. We drown in our heads because we don't take action.

I've spent years stoking the embers of consciousness, intuition, creativity and *being*, but it wasn't until I started to *do* concrete work that I felt truly fulfilled and worthy of respect.

ARE YOU READY TO DO IT?

Coaching clients come to me looking for help identifying and applying their personal gifts. They want to be useful, balanced, and whole (fully developed emotionally, spiritually, physically). They want to be fulfilled. They are a little less afraid of bending social norms than the average Joe or Jane, and have enough self-awareness to be curious about how to use it. In his article, *What if Nobody Was Looking?*, author and founder of *Good Life Project* Jonathon Fields says there are three legs to our awareness "self-stool." The legs, according to him, are: Self-Awareness, Self-Esteem, and Self-Expression.

SO, WE'VE GOT SELF-AWARENESS

Many of my clients are quite conscious and therefore skilled in self-awareness. They are learners and ponderers. They constantly read books, listen to podcasts, explore their minds and hearts, and share their findings with a few cherished companions. They are usually in a transformational period where they have just discovered they have wings or just figured out how to heal their wings from the pinions of a negative relationship. They only need a little encouragement (esteem) and courage to leap into the self-expression chasm.

I understand their position because I've been there. As I said in "Practice One: Waking Up", one drawback to keen self-awareness is critical self-judgment. It's easy to focus on what we're missing when we are overly familiar with all the dark corners of our mind and spirit.

It's hard to find the level of competency that is good enough to stop analyzing and start doing. I spent years figuring out how to be a good personal coach. I spent years dating and looking to meet expectations (mine and my partner's). I didn't get anywhere with either until I actually dug in and did the work. I had to start coaching. I had to commit to a long-term relationship. I stopped theorizing and living by other people's standards and leapt.

SELF-ESTEEM WHEN YOU'RE SENSITIVE AND INTROVERTED

As I said, I was the quiet, obedient older sister who, when not with my closest friends, spent a lot of time alone in my room. My younger sister constantly voiced her mind, joined every team imaginable, and couldn't sit still for long—and when she did, it was rarely alone. My sister received a lot of attention for being bold and extroverted.

As an adult, I understand and appreciate our differences (even recognize many of our similarities), but as a young person I often felt under-heard, hurt, or inferior.

As an introvert and someone with a sensitive nature, it is easy to feel sub-par in our culture. Throughout history it's been the person who is friends with everyone who is revered. Most people admire the doers and the individuals with high energy. Not that introverts aren't capable of leading or can't rally energy for friendships and amazing work, but it takes more effort. We get overwhelmed if the stimulation and energy levels stay high for too long. We have to manage our energy instead of just spilling it all over multiple projects and relationships. Our self-esteem can suffer because of this perceived societal maladaptation.

To make up for my perceived personality deficits, I aligned with strong confident people. I married a man who spoke with conviction, got things done and knew how to network. I tried to mirror his ways or let him run the show. Either way, I forsook authenticity for self-esteem by proxy. It didn't work.

It wasn't until I gained understanding about introversion and met other people like me (who were happy, intuitive and fulfilled) that my self-esteem started to blossom.

They encouraged me and engaged me in things I was enthusiastic and excited about (reading, writing, fitness, making music, talking about spirituality, psychology, personal development, etc.), so much so, that I took action steps to do them and apply them in my life. In doing them, I gained confidence, even if I did not do them well. I gave myself credit for making mistakes and surviving.

Through coaching, I am able to pass on this beautiful practice of self-esteem boosting and self-expression encouragement. Oh my God is it fulfilling! And the best thing is my work requires me to do what I love (reading, research, participating in meaningful conversations) with skills that come naturally, albeit with the right amount of challenge. I am in my element.

SELF-EXPRESSION MEANS DOING WORK OUTSIDE OF YOUR HEAD

I have worked with coaching clients of the Myers–Briggs type preference INTJ. They are industrious folks. They are especially pleased when they accomplish something. They are driven people looking to fulfill a purpose. While working with them I've discovered I have a penchant for completion too. It feels so good to close out a positive coaching session. It makes my heart swell when I tick off all the tasks on my to-do list. I like to work steadily, have structure (sometimes) and reach the end of projects.

> *"If you want anyone to take you seriously, what you really want is their respect. And you can't just be given respect.... You have to earn it. You earn it by doing things that matter, and working on projects that matter and putting in the effort every single day. It's the only way to earn it."* —**Jon Westenberg,** *Stop Trying to Be Somebody*

I tell my clients, "Inspiration + Implementation = Transformation". I got this formula's ingredients from business coach, Jeffrey Shaw of *Creative Warriors Unite*. I strive to integrate this formula into my life. Implementation is by far the toughest component to complete. With my temperament, inspiration is everywhere. I could collect and savor inspiration forever without making anything out of it. Since many of my clients are introverts—and spend a lot of time in their heads or inner worlds—they struggle with interjecting into the external world too. I want the closure of achievement for my clients and myself. I want the respect and satisfaction that comes from expressing through doing. I want to help others transform. I want them to feel fulfilled. This is my purpose. Purpose drives action. Realization of purpose brings transformation.

CARL JUNG AND THE DEVELOPMENT OF THE PSYCHE

Carl Jung believed there was a natural and proper path of development for each individual. It involved paying attention to the inner voice. It involved a striving for unity among the attitudes (introversion and extroversion) and functions of the individual's psyche. While many psychiatrists and psychotherapists of the day focused on interpersonal relationships, Jung focused on the inner psyche. He believed interpersonal relationships were important but could only fully and maturely develop after a person's inner world was reconciled.

Jung proposed the psyche operated by four functions: thinking, feeling, sensation, and intuition. Thinking and feeling are the two functions allocated to making decisions. The former uses logic and reason to problem solve and the latter uses personal values and the effect on people and emotions. Sensation and intuition are the two functions employed to take in information. Sensation uses the five senses and direct facts and input from the environment.

Intuition pulls information from insight, gut feelings and recognition of patterns and general concepts. Although each person used each attitude and function, they were not all used with equal preference and skill. Often a preferred attitude, i.e. introverted or extroverted— the introvert's bias toward the inner world, the extroverts toward the external—and a function dominated or exaggerated behavior and how someone handled an experience. For example, a woman could be an introverted feeler and get lost in her thoughts and emotions and not look for help or logic from the people and information around her. A tension would develop within her and she would need to self-regulate by working on building up the functions and attitude opposite of her natural preferences (i.e. work on extroversion and thinking).

INDIVIDUATION

As we mature, our ability to use appropriate behavior in different situations improves. Jung called this process of unifying and appropriately adapting the components of the psyche *individuation*. Individuation is mature independence. It is a spiritual process of looking inward and synthesizing the conscious (our preferred and dominant functions/attitudes) and unconscious (those functions/ attitudes we do not access easily). Complete balancing and competence in all functions and attitudes is impossible. Jung even said a person with equal adeptness in all functions would be insane. The striving is where the growth occurs.

As mentioned in Practice One, Jung believed the individuation process primarily began in the second half of life after independence from parents, establishment of a family and contribution to society had occurred. Many of Jung's patients had already established themselves with careers and families but were left with a feeling of emptiness. They wanted more meaning in their lives. This neuroticism served as a signal for potential development, unity and wholeness within the individual. Jung was even known to say, "Thank God he became neurotic!" when speaking of a patient on the verge of self-discovery and individuation.

He found these awakening individuals to be one-sided in their preference development. Perhaps, for example, they were too focused on their introverted sensing which presented itself as an exaggerated use of details or memories. Or they exhibited an overuse of their extroverted thinking, which would look like an emphasis on effective problem solving with logic, largely ignoring feelings (theirs and other's). They did not know how to incorporate the opposite attitudes and functions, like extroverted intuition or introverted feeling into their lives. To develop their psyche, they needed to pay attention to their inner world but also exist and contribute to the outer world. It was the therapist's job to help the patient develop the potential capabilities in their non-dominant attitudes and functions.

Therefore, as introverts in Jung's individuation process, we would need to strive to not only thrive in our inner world, but find ways to establish ourselves in the outer, extroverted world as well. If we feel most comfortable relying on facts and concrete information (sensation), we would also need to practice embracing our intuition, the big picture and future possibilities. If we make decisions easily based on our personal values or keeping harmony within the group (both in line with the feeling function), then we would want to work on using intellect, logic and effectiveness (attributes of the thinking function) also.

PERSONAL DEVELOPMENT NOT FOR THE MAJORITY?

Jung believed only exceptional individuals reached the peaks of personal development. Individuation means parting company with the crowd. It could lead to loneliness at first. Most people are more comfortable within the majority. They follow the choices and beliefs of their families, religious affiliations or community.

"The fact that the conventions always flourish in one form or another only proves that the vast majority of mankind do not choose their own way, but convention, and consequently develop not themselves but a method and a collective mode of life at the cost of their own wholeness." —**Carl Jung**

Jung thought only exceptional individuals could tune into their own nature and advance it by developing their personal functions and values. As we said in chapter one, real character develops by working on our weaknesses and losing our egos in the "valley of humility." The road to a higher self means monitoring, confronting and enhancing our internal processes and virtues or lack thereof.

SELF-DISCIPLINE

"The impediment to action advances action.
What stands in the way becomes the way." —**Marcus Aurelius**

Character and wholeness are built by creating constructive habits, desires and lifestyles that defeat our inner weaknesses. According to David Brooks in *The Road to Character*, we become more disciplined, considerate, and loving through a thousand small acts of self-control, sharing, service, friendship and refined enjoyment. Brooks talks about making disciplined, caring choices that create entrenched positive neural pathways. A thousand small acts of self-control sounds like a practice to incorporate like yoga, fitness, or meditation. The benefits do not show up overnight. The practices must be applied consistently and require self-discipline.

Self-discipline is a skill. It is the ability to focus and overcome distractions. It is the ability to make ourselves do what we do not want to do and not do what we want to do. In many cases, it is doing what is right or good for us (or our children, our friends, our spouse, etc.) versus doing what is easy. It requires pause, conscious choice, and delayed gratification.

The things that lead us astray from character development and self-discipline are short-term, like fear, lust or gluttony. Good character traits, such as courage, honesty, perseverance and self-reliance, are long term and the results of self-discipline.

EMOTIONAL AVAILABILITY AND SELF-DISCIPLINE

For those who grew up with little emotional availability or structure from their parents, the struggle is even more difficult. *In Running on Empty: Overcome Your Childhood Emotional Neglect*, psychologist, Dr. Jonice Webb, says clients from emotionally unavailable and permissive homes often come to her with complaints about their procrastination, lack of motivation and disorganization. Their parents, although loving and giving, did not make them do chores around the house. They did not establish set dinner, bed or homework times. The children could eat whatever and whenever they wanted. They could spend money on whatever they wanted. The individual as a child was not truly seen or given limits.

When they grew up, they had no idea how to set limits and accomplish long-range goals themselves. They were used to immediate gratification and indulgence. In other words, they found it difficult to do the things that helped them complete long-term tasks or long-term character development.

In the absence of a parental voice giving the child guidance, structure and discipline, the child developed their own inner voice, which could be hyper-critical — *You idiot! You are going to be late again* or over-indulgent — *That homework doesn't matter. It'll be more fun to watch TV.*

My parents were involved and I had all of my basic needs met. I was never hungry. I had the proper clothing and memorable vacations. My parents exemplified self-discipline regarding work fairly well. They both worked hard. My dad and stepmother taught us how to dust, vacuum, and do dishes. We had meals and bedtimes at regular hours. The thing that trips up my self-discipline regiment now, that could have its roots in my childhood, is the fact that my parents were very "hands-off" once I entered high school when it came to discipline, monitoring my school work or checking in on my emotional life. I did not have a curfew. My homework was my responsibility. They assumed I was toeing the line like I always did, or that I would speak up if I needed anything. Speaking up in general is not easy for an introvert, but speaking up about feelings is even harder.

Soft inquiry regarding my inner thoughts would have been most helpful. It would have given me a feeling of being seen and supported. I don't remember any conversations about my future.

I was on my own to figure that out. Financially, it was difficult for my parents to contribute to post-high school expenses. I watched my friends' parents help them land jobs and make decisions about college. I learned from them.

My mother provided scheduling and home life stability but not a lot of emotional stability. She was always there for food, money, a ride, etc. but she had a lot on her plate and I learned not to bother her. She did not make us do work around the house. She said it was easier to do it herself. She struggled with depression and used food to comfort herself. She had no coping skills and relied on others, food and medication to soothe her discomfort. Sadly, she did not have many loving secure relationships around her to help her deal with life's ups and downs.

My parents' motto was, "We'll give you rope until you hang yourself." They have even told me in recent years they just assumed I was OK. They were happy to not have to worry about me. They could focus on work, other relationships and other endeavors.

Without my parents' consistent guidance and structure, I learned to take care of myself but also developed a longing for someone to help make decisions and notice how great I was at accomplishing things. I stayed fit. Got good grades. Maintained a nice social circle. Worked a job. Paid my way to Spain my senior year of high school. Yet, there was a feeling of unsteadiness. Something missing. I was not truly seen or fully supported. I knew that if I fell, it would be mostly up to me to recover.

My parents' removed style of parenting left me to figure out my own methods of self-discipline. Fortunately, my friends and their families were good influences. I also had a drive to learn new things (which I inherited from my father). I'd had enough success in school to know I wanted a college degree and thus was willing to work toward that goal.

It does not take too much imagination to picture what could have happened if I had not run with ambitious and disciplined friends, had not had parents who modeled good work ethic, or if I'd lacked curiosity. It would have been easy to slip into a life of settling for mediocre. With no one checking on my grades or future, I could have indulged in more television viewing, less homework and studying. I could have eaten my way to comfort, like my mom, and not learned the good feeling of being healthy or the benefit of using positive methods of self-soothing. I could have settled for a high school degree and a career that did not challenge me. In the absence of a parental voice, I could have installed a hypercritical one of my own. I could have paralyzed my actions with a requirement of perfection. I would have been asleep at the wheel, living a reactionary life.

If you are traveling that path now, I recommend waking up, as described in Practice One. Take a proactive lead in your life. Take time to figure out who you are and how to leverage your skills and resources. I also strongly suggest following the steps toward self-discipline spelled out in the following paragraphs.

APPLYING SELF-DISCIPLINE DEFICITS FROM THE PAST

As I said, I was lucky to have the drive and good influences to push me toward my goals. The problem came when I began parenting my own children. I subconsciously administered the same tactics or lack of tactics my parents did. I assumed my kids did not need me involved with their every move. They would figure it out and accomplish independence like I did. The fast-paced world of upper-middle-class suburbia already had me carpooling, volunteering at schools, throwing huge birthday parties and helping with homework a hundred times more than my parents ever did. In their defense, the 70s and 80s were times of freedom, less parental supervision, and less focus on academic perfection.

TECHNOLOGY, PARENTING AND SELF-DISCIPLINE TODAY

In today's culture of busy-ness and meritocracy, it is easy to pass the buck of parenting onto technology, school teachers, and team coaches. We are busy, so our children have to be busy too. We do not have time to give them our undivided attention. The television, iPad, laptop, and phone keep them quiet while we work on our iPad, laptop and phone. We get them to all of their extra-curricular activities and do our best to ensure their future success with tutoring, ACT prep classes, fitness training, etc., but do we ask them how they are feeling? Do they know they are loved and *feel* they are loved? Do we know what lights them up? Do we take the time to play with them or let them play?

As a parent, I know I fail daily in the "be present" department. I am aware of the consequences of emotional neglect and I still falter. In order to get my work done, I let the rules and schedule slide at home. I make more eye contact with my laptop than I do with my kids some days. I reward or entertain my kids with food. I let them take the lead in their welfare by asking them questions such as, "Are you ready for bed now?" and "Do you think you can get your homework done later if you workout/watch TV/play now?" My self-discipline needs improvement. I'm not setting a good example.

In occupational therapist Victoria Prooday's article, "Why Are Our Children So Bored at School, Cannot Wait, Get Easily Frustrated and Have No Real Friends?", she mentions the changes in children and parenting she has seen in her ten years of work. She says technology has disconnected us emotionally from our children and families. Parents are apt to give the child a device rather than offer emotional availability. Technology does not give children emotional warmth and a sense of being heard and seen. It diminishes attention spans with its high stimulation and immediate gratification. Kids want everything to be exciting like their games/videos and they want it now. Doing tedious or effortful work causes meltdowns. Children do not know how to wait or work steadily. They don't have self-discipline.

> *"The concept of 'need to do' is absent."* —**Victoria Prooday**

I started working as a substitute paraprofessional in the public school system last year. As a special-needs paraprofessional, I see the effects of long-term technology babysitting. Granted, there are other causes for attention issues including ADHD and depression, but technology definitely plays a detrimental role. Kids cannot sit still to listen to instructions from the teacher. They need constant redirection to stay on task. Their lives are led by a series of beeps, bells, and chimes. I admit I am guilty of using my Fitbit fitness watch as a reward if a student completed his schoolwork. I will not do that again. Thank you Ms. Prooday for your reminder. My mother, who spent thirty-one years as a pre-school teacher, said that by the end of her tenure she practically had to be Houdini to keep the kids' attention. They do not know how to say no to distractions, especially during tasks that require concentration such as handwriting or timed-testing.

My client's son struggles to get up and ready in the morning. He is a teenager now and better about getting himself around, but since he was in elementary school, he's struggled with time management. Every morning there would be yelling (from his mom unfortunately), half-eaten breakfasts, an unzipped backpack and mad-dashes out the door to catch the bus. No matter what Sarah, my client, did to get him up and motivated, he still managed to fall back asleep after she woke him, dilly-dally in the shower, not have his homework together and raise her blood pressure.

Sarah and her husband are fairly structured and organized people but she has a tendency to grant leniency. With so many things on her to do list, it is difficult to monitor her son's every step. She has more of a "I don't care how you do it, just get it done attitude." Could this be form of, "We'll give you rope until you hang yourself"? Because of Dr. Webb's book, I have asked Sarah to take a deep look at the possibility of emotional neglect as the culprit for her son's lack of self-discipline. Were they overly permissive, leaving him to his own devices too often? Sarah admits having a hard time asking people to do things. Did they focus on his performance more than his feelings, thus giving him a hyper-critical inner voice he can't ignore? These are hard pills to swallow as parents.

Now that their son is considering colleges, it is absolutely necessary to focus on long-term goals. It is difficult to get him to do the (tedious) but necessary steps to work toward completing applications.

In working with him to develop his self-discipline, Sarah and her husband have to apply self-sacrifice mixed with self-control. They need to be a conglomeration of the old eulogy virtues of the early to mid-1900s (patience, generosity, selflessness) and the résumé virtues (drive, tenacity, assertiveness) of the 2000s. They have to offer emotional availability and distinct actions steps to foster his development. In doing so, they stretch their character and his. Whew, it's hard!

Here are recommended action steps for improving children's self-discipline:

- Teach your child to do tedious work like folding laundry or dusting

- Make them wait! They do not have to have the latest toy/ phone/clothing the same day they ask for it. They can wait thirty minutes for dinner without having a snack

- Avoid technology use in cars and restaurants

- Limit constant snacking. They are not hungry all the time, but they eat like they are

- Set limits. Bedtimes, amount of junk food allowed, technology time, meal times. These should all be spelled out

- Social expectations. Encourage eye contact and manners. Make them share things. Have them take turns. Embody the golden rule

- Say no to them and stick to it. It is so easy to appease, but being a parent means doing what's good for our children, not what requires the least effort. Consistency is key. Kids have an incredible knack for wearing us down. I've learned to say "No" with no further explanation. I had to curtail my tendency to justify my negative response. That registered as "the door is not completely closed" to my children. Mom's still talking. She must feel guilty, weak, or open to discuss the request. Say "No" and walk away

We all falter sometimes when it comes to self-discipline. We are human, but if it has been a chronic issue our whole lives, it's time to dig into the causes, take action to remedy the negative outcomes, and improve our overall character.

Dr. Webb says signs of poor self-discipline are:

- We feel that we are lazy

- We procrastinate

- We have difficulty with deadlines

- We tend to overeat, drink too much, oversleep or overspend

- We are bored with the tedium of life

- We tend to avoid mundane tasks

- We are angry at ourselves for how little we get done

- We underachieve

- We are disorganized even though we have the capacity to do better

ANOTHER WAY TO CHANNEL AND DEVELOP SELF-DISCIPLINE

As adults, besides the action steps for children, which also apply to us, there is something else we can do to increase our self-discipline. We can figure out our higher and lower loves. We can reflect on what we value most. If we have a vested interest or belief in what we do, we tend to incorporate habits to support the desired behavior and outcomes. Once we know what we value, the short-term distractions are easier to ignore or replace with healthy choices.

As writer Mark Manson humorously and not so subtly put it in his post, *The Subtle Art of Not Giving a Fuck*, we have to figure out where we want to give a fuck. We only have so many fucks to give and not giving a fuck (indifference) is not an option. Not giving a fuck—meaning we do not mind being different—is good. If we are willing to go against the crowd and put time and energy into what matters to us instead of what matters to the crowd, we will go somewhere.

How do we figure out what we value most? A minister I know once asked, "What breaks your heart enough to make you stand up and fight?" It could go the other way too. "What fills your heart enough to make you stand up and fight?" Ranking our desires and loves based on morals can help us stay disciplined. For example, love for our children is a higher love than our love of web surfing or a favorite television show. Therefore, organizing our self-discipline based on our love for our children is a priority. Internet surfing and television viewing, are things we can limit to enhance our relationships with our kids. Activities and behaviors that improve or support our highest loves keep us on the right track by helping us say "No" to those that do not.

What are some of your highest priorities? Your community? A charity or cause you serve? Your pets? How can they help you say "Yes" to the things you do not want to do and "No" to the things you do (that are not beneficial)?

I will give credit to fitness and a workout routine for improving my self-discipline. It helped to have my husband, trainer, and friends hold me accountable for making it to the gym, but once I started to see and feel results, it was easy to take over and continue the mental and physical benefits. Making fitness a part of my self-care forces me to schedule and say "No" to activities that are not a higher love. Fitness also, by its very nature, requires us to do things we do not want to do. Getting up early in the morning, doing five more leg presses, or running one more mile? All challenges we could easily say "No" to but we don't. We push through and finish the workout, giving us a hit of dopamine and norepinephrine along the way. Self-respect and self-esteem blossom during regular physical activity too.

WHERE TO START WHEN YOU HAVE NO DISCIPLINE?

What if your life is one big indulgent, disorganized and stressful mess? What if you have no self-discipline? Where do you start? You start small. Do one small additional task every day. For instance, decide to never leave dirty dishes in the sink overnight, and then make sure the sink is empty before you go to bed every night for a week. Make your bed every day for a week. It may help to make an X or a check mark each day on the calendar when you complete the chosen task. This gives you an extra feeling of accomplishment.

Think about what drives you morally. What do you value highly? A mature and morally driven person strives to spread more light than darkness. They work to further projects that can never be completed in a lifetime. They have personal truths that drive them. They are always working to better themselves. Considering and including these lofty ideals into our everyday existence, gives us signposts to follow and strength to carry us as we embody self-discipline.

This morning, I knew I had to spend all day and most of the night working on this chapter of the book. I knew it was going to require strict discipline. No talking with friends on the phone. No mindless eating as I type. No extensive breaks. I set a goal of writing 4,200 words by six o'clock. Writing and sharing helpful insight (self-expression) are two of my higher loves. They give me the purpose and energy to work steadily and put off distractions.

I hit my target word count at the six o'clock deadline. I did not stray from my work today. By doing so, I boosted my self-esteem and self-respect. Add that to new self-awareness and my self-table (more legs than a stool) is pretty stable. There's a feeling of self-reliance and self-confidence that self-discipline (wow! that's a lot of selfs) breeds. There's healing in completing projects and expressing ourselves.

CREATIVITY AS HEALER

"Always the seer is a sayer. Somehow his dream is told; somehow he publishes it with solemn joy: sometimes with pencil on canvas, sometimes with chisel on stone, sometimes in towers and aisles of granite, his soul's worship is built; sometimes in anthems of indefinite music, but clearest and most permanent, in words." —**Ralph Waldo Emerson**

Jung used a technique he called *active imagination* with his patients. He encouraged them to enter a state of reverie in which there was no judgment and no interference from him. Active imagination sounds a lot like the flow state, or meditation doesn't it? Within active imagination patients told of their fantasies. Jung suggested they paint or draw these fantasies as they bubbled to the surface of their consciousness. While creating, the patients re-discovered parts of themselves long forgotten or hidden. Jung believed the unconscious held the secrets to our wholeness. He often used dream interpretation and active imagination to bring the unconscious to light.

I often use intuitive writing with my coaching clients. The uncensored, free flow of writing based on prompts also brings up neglected or underused aspects of the client's psyche. It helps bring unity between the conscious and unconscious, the internal and external world, just as Jung's active imagination did.

In asking my coaching clients where they feel most alive and most at home, I help them recall what makes life meaningful. Sometimes it leads them to take up a hobby or passion they abandoned to meet the demands of an achievement and competition-based world.

One client, who is fully aware of the benefits and healing found in creating art, often paints pictures with a woman in them. The woman is always her, and post-painting she makes a point of interpreting what the piece tells her about herself. One time she knew she had to paint a picture in black-and-white with shades of grey. When interpreting the painting after it was finished, she realized she had been trying to live her life too strictly—in matters of black and white. She started to look at and create "grey" options in her life too.

UNDERSTANDING LIVES AT THE INTERSECTION OF UNCONSCIOUS AND CONSCIOUS

Those with a creative talent are often better able to bridge the gap between the external reality and the inner world. A writing teacher once told our class to make the universal specific within our writing. I pondered this idea for a while. She wanted us to link our own specific experience with that of the universe or that of others. In doing so we create understanding. At the intersection of our psyche and the external world there is connection and understanding. For example, I might write about a time when my children were embarrassed to have me speak in their school about introversion. The idea of being ashamed about introversion and its traits may resonate with my readers. Putting my feelings and insight about introversion out into the world serves as a gateway between the unconscious and conscious.

Often a hunger to create unity within our chaotic and unbalanced psyche propels us to investigate and create external manifestations. We want understanding. We want to resonate with others. Do artists have an advantage when it comes to healing from past wounds or depression?

GRIEF AND LOSS. HOW THEY AFFECT SELF-ESTEEM AND SELF-DISCIPLINE

A study done on children who lost their mother at an early age (before eleven) showed they had a greater chance of suffering severely from a mental illness later in life. It was the severity of the mental illness that was unique to the children who experienced grief from death of a parent. It was not the appearance of mental illness itself.

It makes sense that children who lost their mother at an early age would experience reduced self-esteem. Mothers are generally the givers of unconditional love and affection in the early stages of our lives. Mothers make children feel loved just for being themselves. Their death (absence) or even a lack of a warm relationship between parent and child can lead to a predisposition for depression for the child later in life.

The lack of an internalized parental voice not only affects self-esteem; it also affects self-discipline as we noted earlier. Self-esteem is not only linked with unconditional love, it is also linked with feelings of competence. It would again make sense that the loss of a parent at an early age would reduce self-esteem and produce a feeling of incompetence or helplessness. Emotional anxiety and depression both come with feelings of powerlessness and helplessness. Women who lost their mothers before age ten were more likely to exhibit dependent or anxiously attached behavior as adults than women who had not lost their mothers.

ARTISTS AND INTROVERTS HAVE AN ADVANTAGE?

Stay with me. I know this is a complex subject. The creatively gifted who suffer from bereavement or depression are often able to use their talents in a process of repair that allows them to come to terms with their loss or pain rather than deny or avoid it. As we discussed the benefits of solitude in Practices One and Two, it was suggested that introverts and the creative process are at home in the solitary environment. The introspective and the creative use solitude and their artistic skills to come to terms with their pain. While others rely on the counsel of others to help them process suffering, the creative and introverted do it within their own psyches. Once the project or art is created, it may be shared with the world, thus bringing the internal external, making the specific, universal.

FINDING CONTROL AND COMPETENCE THROUGH CREATIVITY

The creative act defies helplessness. It gives the creator a feeling of control and competence. It pushes hopelessness aside. It serves as a coping mechanism and as a method of expressing emotion. As we learned in Practice Two, naming or labeling emotions is a powerful tool to combat anxiety. It moves our neural processes from the primitive and reactive limbic system to the more evolved and controlled prefrontal cortex.

Creating art is not exactly labeling emotions, but it is expressing them in an organized way. It gives us a narrative and formulated way of describing our feelings. No unconditional love or parental voice can lead to low self-esteem and little to no self-discipline. If we work on and complete long-term creative projects, we improve both.

Anthony Storr, therapist and author of *Solitude: A Return to the Self*, says, "The search for order, for unity, for wholeness is, I believe, a motivating force of signal importance in the lives of men and women of every variety of temperament. The hunger for imagination is active in every human being to some degree. But the greater the disharmony within, the sharper the spur to seek harmony, or if one has the gifts, to *create* harmony."

Perhaps it is a blessing to be neurotic?

WHAT DRIVES US TO DEVELOPMENT AND WHOLENESS?

What is it that compels some of us to struggle to achieve wholeness and not others? What drives a portion of us to apply self-discipline and create expressions of our feelings? Jung argued it is not necessity, for necessity still leads most people to follow conventions. He also said it is not moral decision because that can still be reinforced by common conventions and traditions and hence be employed by the majority.

Jung called it vocation or a calling. In its essence it is a combination of what we long to do and what the world needs us to do. This drives us to complete ourselves, to develop our inner being and release it into the world. It calls us to transform.

Inspiration + Implementation = Transformation

Jung believed unity of the psyche or wholeness is not sustainable. The end point of individuation, where the fragments of our psyche unify, feels like being one with the universe and resembles a sense of peace, but the nature of humans is to continuously change. We get comfortable in a setting, then a tension or change occurs and we have to adapt to create the feeling of unity and harmony within again. So, in this way, we are always stretching and growing to achieve wholeness. We need difficulties to nudge us. We need the quieting of the ego and the humility of the struggle to advance our growth.

If we do not listen and let our difficulties or imbalances nudge us, we risk overdeveloping certain traits. Anything overdone is problematic. For example, if we do not check our natural preference for critiquing over appreciating (a Thinking preference), we may alienate loved ones with our perceived negativity.

If we do allow for humility, self-examination and growth, we add to our wisdom and maturity. This maturity was not won by competing with others but by improving ourselves through self-discipline and healing ourselves through self-expression. The fragmented pieces of our psyche, and the confusion about what or who to follow, settle into a wholeness led by higher loves and a deep calling.

CHALLENGES TO BECOMING WHOLE

If we are depressed or our lives are chaotic, it is tough to develop self-discipline. The idea of organizing and taking control seems overwhelming. We do not have to be depressed or severely disorganized to lack self-discipline either. Sometimes we just enjoy being in our head and collecting data so much that we forget to make a move.

Action steps for integrating self-discipline:

1. Start small. Do one small task every day that you do not want to do but gives you immediate results. For example, make your bed every morning. If you forget or run out of time one day, do not beat yourself up about it. You have not failed. Simply make

the bed as soon as you can that day, even if it is right before you crawl into it at night. You only fail if you give up altogether and stop doing it.

2. List your higher loves. What goals, people, causes, or projects feel right when you work on them? Think about those that have long-term benefits. They give you the most reward.

3. Stop the reverie and put your big-girl or -boy pants on. There is no transformation without implementation. Personal development is hard, and only a few have the courage, guts, chutzpah, endurance, etc. to do it. Listen for your calling and let nothing get in your way. When you slip up, do not soothe yourself with indulgences like food, drugs, alcohol, shopping, Internet surfing, television, co-miserable friends, etc. Just begin again.

We are challenged if we are too one-sided with our preferences and do not spend time honing the other functions within our psyche. We feel an imbalance or tension within us.

Action steps for unifying the different attitudes and functions of your psyche:

1. Have a therapist, personal coach or friend help you figure out your dominant functions—the ones you have been doing without prompting since you were a child. Listen for words like stupid, idiotic, or love to come out of your mouth. These signal a bias in your thinking or feeling. Consider choosing an action that would surprise someone close to you and is the opposite of your bias. Perhaps you love to problem solve using logic. It is the only thing that makes sense to you. You believe people who use emotions to guide them are *idiots*. Next time an issue comes up turn to your heart or other people's hearts first to

help you make a decision and resolve the issue. If you rarely use your senses or body to engage with the world, try taking a fitness class or playing a musical instrument. Physically, challenge yourself. As an introvert, it is easy to stay inside our heads, strive to bring what is inside you out into the world. If you love to read for example, find a friend or book club to share favorite books or authors with. I suggest meeting face-to-face. Interactions on the Internet will not give you that stretch of growth necessary to improve neglected functions.

SECTION III:
INTERDEPENDENCE

In Section I, we discussed the dependence phase of the maturity continuum and its reliance on the influences and approval of others. We said via Stephen Covey, "*Dependence* is the paradigm of *you—you* take care of me; *you* come through for me; *you* didn't come through; I blame *you for the results.*"

At the dependence maturity level, control is in another person's hands. We allow others to take care of us physically. They make decisions for us or influence our thinking intellectually. If we are emotionally dependent, we depend on others to improve our moods and give us a sense of security and self-worth.

For introverts, that often means we undervalue our nature because society values high-energy, friendly, fun, talkative, outgoing, popular people. It means we adjust our demeanor to align with the external world's expectations. We put on our active, vocal, group-friendly masks and do our best to fit in.

As we move away from the dependence phase, we move into independence. Covey said independence is the paradigm of *I. I* can do it. *I* am responsible for myself. *I* choose my path.

We move into and through our independence by noticing tensions pushing us to change. These elements of discomfort may be internal or external, positive or negative, but they cause us to wake up and become conscious of our living.

Through reflection and time in solitude it is easier to hear our inner voice. We make thoughtful decisions and consider our dearest relationships. We don't have to worry about being perfect or falling short of other's expectations. In solitude, we find ourselves.

By slowing down and paying attention, our natural inclinations and preferences surface. Creativity blooms as we have time to notice beauty and our five senses. Ideas percolate and develop as we give them time to play out. There is a clarity that helps us self-direct. We no longer need others to lead us. We have a better understanding of what drives us, what we are willing to work for.

Another ingredient that fosters our independence is someone or a group of significant people who believe in us. They do not judge us. They do not indulge us. They provide a mirror to show us what we are capable of and whom we are. They serve as role models and they serve as support.

The support of nonjudgmental peers and the self-awareness and calming presence found in our element, give us the courage to take action outside of our comfort zones. The inspiration pushes us to act. Self-discipline improves and our self-respect rises. We not only think about ideas, we implement them. We transform.

We begin a process of unifying our inner psyche by working on preferences and cognitive functions (thinking, feeling, sensing, intuition) we largely neglected in the past. We have a desire to become whole. As introverts, we may strive to put ourselves out into the world more—get out of our heads and into our bodies or into activities and interactions outside of our inner realm. If we are predominant users of group harmony and feelings to make decisions, we may start to incorporate logic and reason into our process.

Our knowledge of our nature, values, flaws, and how we contribute leads to increased self-confidence. The more inner-directed we are the more capable we are of building and healing relationships.

Stephen Covey defined maturity as courage plus consideration. Courage is necessary to carry out full-blown authenticity. Vulnerability and willingness to go against the grain take bravery. Living authentically while taking others' perspectives and feelings into consideration is maturity.

As introverted, highly sensitive or socially anxious people, we may struggle with the courage piece. Assertiveness is not easy. We tend to think of it as a version of aggressiveness. Aggressiveness feels harsh and loud.

What if we thought of assertiveness as a diplomatic way to get our message across so the other person can take it in with minimum discomfort? Diplomacy is not so bad. Diplomacy allows us to stay thoughtful and tender, while expressing our needs.

We need character and independence to move into interdependence. We saw the rise of personality and competition as gauges for a person's worth starting in the early 1900s with the movement of people from rural areas to urban settings. But based on psychobiological research, neuroscience and personal experience with clients and my own life, I propose that the most fulfilling and rich lives come from what Stephen Covey calls the *laws of life*: self-discipline, integrity, cooperation, and contribution. Tapping into our values, self-respect, and self-awareness (gleaned during our work toward independence) while taking part in healthy relationships is the ultimate maturity. This is interdependence.

An interdependent person has the ability to share him or herself meaningfully and has access to the vast resources of others. Each person is maximized in their potential to care for themselves, but maximized even further by the addition of what the other person has to offer.

Dr. Jonice Webb, psychologist and author of *Running on Empty*, defines mutual interdependence as when both parties in a relationship are capable of a healthy level of independence and self-reliance, but each person relies on the other for some things at sometimes. Each person is maximized in their potential to care for themselves, but maximized even further by the addition of what the other person has to offer.

Out in the world, we discover how interdependent we are. It is necessary to advocate for ourselves and rely on others' contributions to our well-being. We take responsibility for our actions and expect accountability and respect from others. Our friends give us warm companionship and trust but we have to earn it by being responsive and consistent with them. Our employers pay us in exchange for our skills and effort. Romantic relationships offer love, growth, and a safe place to be ourselves but those gifts are the by-product of effort, patience and understanding.

Most of us flourish when we feel supported. The sum is far greater than its parts in mature interdependence.

Practice Four: Getting Past Independence Principles of Love and Relationship

"We might think that knowing ourselves is a very ego-centered thing, but by beginning to look so clearly and so honestly at ourselves — at our emotions, at our thoughts, at who we really are — we begin to dissolve the walls that separate us from others." **— Pema Chodron,** *To Know Yourself is to Forget Yourself*

One spring, I focused on working on the outside of my house. There were maintenance issues inside as well, but the big projects happened outside. I had the deck restained. I had the shake repainted, and cleaned up the landscaping. The outside work ran parallel to my then new views on living and loving. I began to see that to have healthy self-esteem, the outside world had to be cared for as much as the inner.

I'd spent the previous few years working on accepting myself and justifying solitude. I thought I was bolstering my self-esteem by gaining self-awareness and validating my sensitive nature. I gained understanding and knowledge, but my self-esteem didn't fully rise until I *applied* that understanding to relationships and meaningful work—both entities outside of my heavily analyzed and prized, inner realm.

INTROVERT FEELS COMPETENT IN THE OUTSIDE WORLD

Psychotherapist Nathaniel Branden (in 1969) defined self-esteem as *"the experience of being competent to cope with the basic challenges of life and being worthy of happiness."* As a sensitive introvert, it takes courage to push myself into the external world, but when I do, I feel truly alive and fulfilled. Dealing with the outside world is a basic challenge of life for the deeply introspective.

Our inner world feels so safe and the outer world bombards us with stimuli and emotional energy. I spend a good portion of my coaching time helping clients gain personal power to manage energy and the two worlds—inner and outer.

NURTURING RELATIONSHIPS HELP WITH CONFIDENCE

As relationship coach Bruce Muzik says in his post, "Fuck Self Love", we build lasting self-esteem by cultivating nurturing relationships with supportive people. The truth in this has become clear to me over the years. My self-worth plummeted when I was not in a nurturing relationship.

For a while, I only had a few people who offered supportive and nurturing companionships. That was when I went deeply internal and studied myself. I don't think this was a bad move—I learned so much—but in the end, it left things unbalanced. I focused intently on my own feelings without applying them to anything. Even when I started writing, the self-expression was heavenly but still missing that fortifying real interaction with the environment and people.

I needed a more hands on way to contribute to the community.

Once I reached out with coaching, I not only felt validated, I felt more confident. I genuinely felt I added value to the world and was worthy of love and happiness. The act of using my skills made me feel competent and purposeful. By building secure and nonjudgmental relationships with my clients, I help them feel confident and competent as well—a win/win.

Dr. Elaine Aron, author of the *Highly Sensitive Person* series, mentioned a study she and her husband, Dr. Arthur Aron and their colleagues conducted with ninety-six individuals found in the top and bottom quartiles of the Sensory Processing Sensitivity Scale. In the study, the subjects rated their arousal level when viewing emotionally evocative and neutral pictures selected from the International Affective Picture System.

High SPS (sensory processing sensitivity) individuals rated pictures eliciting emotion, especially positive emotion, as significantly more attractive (positively valanced) and tended to respond faster to the positive pictures; also, high SPS individuals who had reported having high-quality parenting reported greater arousal in response to positive pictures.

Overall, results suggest that high SPS individuals respond more strongly to emotional stimuli—especially positive stimuli—without being more aroused unless they had especially high-quality parenting, in which case they were more positively aroused.

> *"This is the second result to show that we respond more to positive than negative stimuli, helping to explain our 'differential susceptibility'—that we do worse in poor environments, true, but better than others in good ones, apparently because we pick up on and process more of the positive experiences in our life."* —Dr. Elaine Aron

No matter how much I love myself through self-awareness, self-care, and self-soothing, I am still going to crave connection. There's a draw toward emotions and humanity. We aren't meant to be in isolation. Even people especially sensitive to stimuli (many introverts) need and desire interaction to grow and thrive.

Introverts and extroverts consciously (and subconsciously) absorb feedback from people in our environment. This affects our confidence. It makes sense that we'd want positive people in our environment to foster our growth. Of course, this needs to be a two-way street. We need to offer support and responsiveness as well.

I'm not so idealistic (but I'm pretty idealistic) to believe we can only have positive feedback in our world. We need constructive feedback too. Those into nurturing (love + care + help) give criticism with diplomacy and actionable steps.

HARD TO SAY WE NEED SOMEONE

I've written a lot about loving yourself first before you can love another. I've encouraged being your own amazing boyfriend and love affairs with solitude. I've been embarrassed to say I wanted or needed someone. I still have attachments to those ideas but more and more I see the power of growing through relationships.

As a staunch advocate for solitude, autonomy, making yourself happy, and the right to be gloriously content as a single person, it was difficult for me to consider putting a romantic relationship first, before my needs and ideals.

After my divorce, I was determined not to settle for anything less than pure magic when it came to my next relationship. I wanted the heady, perfect, romantic, sexy, intelligent, steadfast lover who could keep me on cloud nine mentally, spiritually, and physically. Of course, that did not work.

One day I caught Dr. Stan Tatkin, Doctor of Psychology and couples therapist, on Jayson Gaddis' *Smart Couple Podcast*. His main message? Put your relationship first. Partners must depend on each other. They are in each other's care. For a secure relationship, the couple team comes first before children, job, performance, appearance, friends, pets, everything and everyone. Your job is to comfort and soothe your partner. You need to know everything about them to understand/alleviate their distress and foster their growth. Their job is to do the same for you. No matter what, you are a team and together you are better than you could be on your own.

After several short unsuccessful relationships and one long-term (but ultimately ended) relationship, I decided perhaps I had been wrong in my approach. I had been, as Dr. Tatkin says, pro-self instead of pro-relationship. I had expectations for my partner and spent a lot of time making sure my needs were spelled out and met instead of focusing on creating a secure relationship. My pro-self-behavior involved pointing out where my partner fell short. Pro-relationship behavior would have worked to gain understanding about his and my behavior.

My battle cry to be magnificently independent and solitude-seeking was based on my fear of being dependent on someone (and being used or let down) and my introverted and creative nature. I wanted love, but no one had soothed me or put me first in a long time. And honestly, I had not done that for anyone else in a long time either.

Dr. Tatkin's words, and scientific data to back them, made it OK to rely on someone. I did not have to be tough and self-reliant all the time. My attitude about dependency within a relationship shifted.

I began to strive for interdependence, that lovely existence where individual integrity ebbs and flows with dependency.

HOW TO KNOW IF WE ARE DEVELOPING AS HUMANS

I consider personal development, particularly for an intuitive introvert, the transformation from a superficially focused being -> to one willing to explore their complete inner world -> to one interested in reaching out and creating nurturing and supportive relationships. In the end, internal and external worlds unite and form a mature being who meets their own needs and those of others.

As introverts, it's oh so easy to retreat into our shells. We will always need solitude and downtime, but the real growth and power comes from sticking our necks out and improving our connection with the outside world.

Making improvements on the exterior of my home changed my focus and gave me a different kind of satisfaction, one not based on my inner world but one shared with those around me.

ARE WE SEPARATE OR RELATIONAL BEINGS?

Hungarian physician and psychoanalyst, Dr. Margaret Mahler's *separation-individuation theory* (not to be confused with Carl Jung's individuation process) stipulates that to grow—beginning in infancy—we have to move further and further away from others. The mature person does not need others. They are a self-contained unit. In fact, the separate-self model has us intrinsically motivated to create firm boundaries between others and us. It states our nature is to gain power over others and compete for limited resources. Sounds like life in the meritocracy, doesn't it?

Dr. Amy Banks, psychiatrist and author of *Wired to Connect*, suggests that mutuality or interdependent connecting (*the relational cultural theory*) is the more natural human inclination. She argues our brains and nervous systems are designed to move us toward more relational complexity. Studies using fMRI show the same part of our brain that lights up when we feel physical pain reacts when we feel social exclusion. Healthy social inclusion tells our brain to stop the stress response.

Within the relational cultural theory people come together, experience each other and then move away in order to absorb what was learned. There is flexibility and an ebb and flow to our mutuality. It allows us to see ourselves and the other person more deeply. It enhances our personal growth by strengthening positive neuropathways and processes through repetition.

In a growth-fostering relationship, we are not denigrated or silenced. We don't have to put our guard up. We are free to develop clarity, boost our self-worth, become more productive, and move toward other fulfilling relationships.

In fact, in patient/therapist relationships where relational cultural theory is practiced, the therapist does not remain reserved or withhold personal experiences, thoughts and evolution. The patient and therapist work together and form a bond.

ARE WE DISTRAUGHT BECAUSE WE DO NOT HAVE ENOUGH BOUNDARIES AND INDEPENDENCE OR BECAUSE WE DO NOT HAVE ENOUGH CONNECTIONS WITH OTHERS?

According to the Anxiety and Depression Association of America, anxiety disorders affect 18% or 40 million people of the US adult population. Of those 40 million people, almost 7 million of them suffer from generalized anxiety disorder, 15 million suffer from social anxiety disorder, 14.8 million suffer from major depressive disorder, and 7.7 million are affected by posttraumatic stress disorder.

How many of those who suffer from anxiety or depression are introverts? That is not known exactly, but a study done by members of the Department of Psychiatry at the University of North Carolina at Chapel Hill in 2001 found suicidal affective disorder patients were significantly more introverted than non-suicidal affective disorder patients.[3] Other studies show isolation as both a cause and effect of depression. With our sensitive nervous systems, society's preference for extroversion and our penchant for alone time, it is a fair assumption we make up a good percentage of those suffering.

After learning of the separation-individuation theory and the relational cultural theory (which has growth and healing occur through human connections), I wondered if anxious and depressed people—many of them introverts—are distraught because they do not have enough independence and personal boundaries or if they are distraught because they do not feel connected to others.

Dr. Banks and many studies point to a sense of belonging and companionship as antidotes to stress and potions for positive well-being.

A large and long-term study started in the 1940s and done at Johns Hopkins involved 1,100 male medical students (all healthy at the start of the study). They were asked how close they felt to their parents. They were tracked down fifty years later. Those who had developed cancer since the start of the study, were less likely to have close relationships with their parents than those who did not have cancer. The correlation, not necessarily the scientific causation, demonstrates the importance of positive relationships to our health. Interestingly, the lack of a close relationship between a male student and his father was the strongest predictor of cancer. These findings were gathered after eliminating known cancer risk factors.[4]

Another particularly intriguing study done at Yale University, looked at cardio angiographs of 119 men and forty women. Cardioangiographs tell whether our coronary arteries are blocked and if so, to what extent. The patients who reported more "feelings of being loved" had far fewer blockages than those who did not. Interestingly, the patients who felt loved had even fewer blockages than the patients who reported having busy social circles but didn't feel particularly nurtured or supported, thus giving credence to the idea that positive nurturing relationships are more powerful than superficial relationships. It should be noted that the angiography study took into consideration genetic disposition for heart disease and any known environmental risk factors.[5]

Put this together with the study mentioned in Practice Three about children who lost their mother at an early age showing warm relationships are vital to our self-esteem and self-discipline, and we have an excellent argument for the necessity of good caring relationships.

Dr. Tatkin says from a psychobiological perspective, most people need to feel closeness and ongoing connection with another human being. We need other people. We can't do it ourselves. Relationships with others reduce our stress and enrich our lives. Another person can understand us, amplify our enthusiasm and joy, provide guidance, make us more productive, help when we are in trouble, motivate us to be more than we are on our own, touch our souls, and, as we will see in Practice Five, heal past wounds.

COUNTER-DEPENDENCE

We know complete dependence on others to help us physically, emotionally, spiritually, and intellectually is at the far-left end of the maturity continuum. It leaves the locus of control in other people's hands. We all start out this way as children, but as we grow and mature we move to independence.

The practice for this chapter is to get beyond independence and embrace relationships or interdependence. Now, independence is more mature than dependence because it means we are not completely influenced and reliant on others. We make our own decisions, take care of ourselves physically, are emotionally inner directed and find self-worth from within.

Many of you may have heard the term codependent. Codependency has its roots in the "Alcoholics Anonymous" program. Codependency is a type of dysfunctional helping relationship where one person supports or enables another person's drug addiction, alcoholism, gambling addiction, poor mental health, immaturity, irresponsibility, or underachievement. The codependent relationship requires the participants to rely on each other's approval for their sense of identity. It sounds a lot like dependency but it is two-way and involves the dysfunctional element that perpetuates addiction, poor mental health or underachievement.

The majority of you have probably not heard the term *counter-dependence*. Mental health professionals mostly use it. Counter-dependent people avoid asking for help, prefer to be completely self-reliant and have a fear of dependency. They will do whatever it takes to avoid needing someone.

What causes counter-dependence? Usually, a message we receive early on from our parents that says, "You're on your own. Learn to be fiercely independent." Sometimes a parent is absent as is the case with a death, deployment, or divorce. Sometimes the parent is there but not really there, such as when parents have issues with chemical dependency and depression or a parent is a workaholic. Sometimes the parent is just overly permissive, not willing to establish and enforce rules, and leaves the child to his own devices. In any case, a sense of the importance of being self-reliant develops. That aversion to dependency gets carried into adulthood and applied to any relationships the individual aspires to create. Unfortunately, healthy long-term relationships require independence and the ability to rely on or trust someone else.

SIGNS OF COUNTER-DEPENDENCE

- Resist or avoid asking for help

- Prefer to do things yourself

- Find intimate relationships difficult

- Need to be right all the time

- Expect perfection in yourself and others

- Find it difficult to relax, like to keep busy

- Avoid anything that makes you appear vulnerable

Counter-dependence robs us of the gift of interdependence. Without interdependence, we never know what it is like to love and feel loved. We miss out on the comfort others bring. When we can't or don't ask for help, we often don't receive it. Others never lessen our burdens. Our fear or plain lack of understanding regarding needing others holds us back from the richness and depth of a mutually interdependent life.

As a parent with counter-dependent tendencies, we feed our children the same message our parents fed us. We subconsciously tell them it is not OK to depend on others. It is most acceptable to take care of ourselves. Needing others is for wimps.

To avoid doing that, we need to show our children we are there for them, consistently. We need to show it is all right to rely on others. No one is belittled or judged for expressing a need for help. It is safe to ask for it.

Examples of ways to be there for our children:

- Maintain rituals or routines in the morning and at bedtime. Wake them up gently and have breakfast with them. Tuck them in at night and take a few minutes to listen to their concerns about the day

- Be around to offer assistance with homework. Let them do the work but be there if they do not understand it and need clarification. Quiz them for tests and help edit papers

- Ask them about their ideas and future plans

- Make something together in the garage or in the kitchen

- Eat dinner together every night. Make the dinner table a safe space to share good news and bad

- Give hugs often

There is a small chance helping our children too much or too often causes a problem, but that only happens if we help them when they do not truly need us.

HELPING VERSUS RESCUING

My daughter is the youngest and only girl among my children. There have been many instances throughout the years, that I have felt the need to protect her from her older brothers. My sons are strong guys with sharp intelligence and occasionally sharp tongues.

My daughter is often the easy target and butt of their jokes. Her tender-hearted spirit and eagerness to join her brothers' team only widen the chasm between them. My penchant to stick up for the underdog flares when I witness any apparent injustices between my sons and her.

In many ways, I am sure this dynamic reminds me of the harsh relationship I had with my sister as a girl. I have a fierce need to protect my daughter from feeling the way I did when my sister and I fought.

After many occasions when I ran interference, my sons made it clear they felt I favored my daughter. No matter what they did or she did, I would side with her.

In the past, because I found it difficult to hear negative remarks and criticism, I developed a knee-jerk reaction to every bit of feedback my sons dished out. To me it sounded like constant put-downs. To their more logical and less emotional minds, it was the truth and even sometimes meant as helpful feedback. In one case, they honestly believed they were saving my daughter from ridicule by telling her the t-shirt she decorated and wore was ugly.

At some point, I stumbled across an article describing the problem with rescuing people. In essence, if we perpetually rescue someone, we are telling him or her we have no faith in their abilities to take care of themselves. It is a vote of no confidence.

With my daughter, I stood back and observed the next few times my sons interacted with her. I saw her respond on her own and I saw her react and look for me to step in. I decided to stop jumping in and speaking for her every time her brothers teased her. I am mindful of the psychological damage of repeated verbal assaults and would not let that happen, of course. But instead of rescuing her, I helped her gather tools to prevent her from feeling like a victim. I gave her funny, albeit corny phrases like, "Buzz off" or "Go jump in a lake" to use when they were being pests. The boys made fun of the phrases, but at least a shift in focus occurred and changed the direction of the conversations. I told her she could always leave the room. She does not have to stand and take it. She can turn away and walk out. I also suggested using humor to earn their admiration. I know how hard it is to throw out funny one-liners when your feelings are hurt (as an introvert, it's hard to throw out one-liners off-the-cuff, period), but if she can do it, the mood in the room will definitely change for the better. Giving her tools instead of a bailout gave her power.

KNOWING WHEN TO FOSTER INTERDEPENDENCE

How can we tell if our children really need us or if it is a good opportunity to let them work through something on their own? The best way to help your child is to stay in tune with him or her. Attachment theory (which we will discuss in Practice Five), says healthy parent/child relationships require an emotional connection with our child. We must pay attention to the child and make sure we are sensitive to his needs and meet them as quickly as possible. For example, expecting a six-year-old to take care of and entertain himself after school is unreasonable. An emotionally in tune parent would know their child needs parental supervision and a chance to talk about their day. They would be there at the end of the day with their child or make arrangements for someone else to care for him or her.

Parents are not perfect. We will fail to help our children occasionally, but if we sincerely try to be there, our children will feel it. As they grow up, they will know it is acceptable to reach out to others when needed. They will have skills for independence and the ability to ask for assistance when needed.

As a personal coach, I have had to learn how to help clients come to their own solutions through a process called *motivational interviewing*. In motivational interviewing, active and reflective listening are employed. I listen to my client tell their story and then rephrase their words as I repeat them back to them. I may include an emotion I sensed in their words and ask if that is indeed what they are feeling. I repeat what seem to be the options or points causing them distress. I let them hear the conflicting options and pause to ponder the best choice. I let them sit in their ambivalence and take care not to offer answers. This is harder than it sounds. Offering solutions or suggestions is just another form of rescuing. If they come to their own conclusions, the action steps needed to resolve the issues are more likely to be carried out. The client feels empowered.

Instead of making my daughter or my clients dependent on me or codependent on me, I create an interdependent relationship with them. They have a healthy dependency on me but also the skills to take care of themselves. The parent/child relationship is largely dependent in that the child has to rely on the adult to take care of her, but as the child matures it is natural for them to develop independence and the ability to ask for help. If they have been able to comfortably depend on their parent then they will hopefully feel at ease being interdependent within future relationships.

WE HAVE TO LOVE OURSELVES FIRST?

We've all heard variations of the saying that we have to love ourselves before we can love another. We at least need to like ourselves and we can't like ourselves if we don't know and respect ourselves. We know ourselves by finding our element, spending time reflecting and paying attention as we said in Practice One. We respect ourselves by exhibiting self-mastery and self-discipline, as mentioned in Practice Three. Stephen Covey says self-mastery and self-discipline are the foundation of good relationships with others.

Why is this? Inevitably, tough times descend upon a relationship. If we do not have the inner-security, self-awareness, proactivity, and self-discipline of a truly independent person, we may regress to comforting addictions, finger pointing, or simply giving up and leaving the relationship. Our personal integrity gives us the grit, the values to prioritize, and the strong character to stick through the rough spots. If we only have relational skills that help us gain power over others or achieve material rewards, i.e. résumé virtues, we will not know how to dig deep and access our eulogy virtues. Eulogy virtues are created and uncovered as we experience independence and important relationships. Knowing and liking ourselves gives us the stability to create effective relationships.

A client of mine learned the value of independent maturity when about six months into a new relationship she received a work assignment that would take her out-of-state 50% of each week for months. She knew her absence could have a dramatic negative effect on the relationship. The time away would be lonely and take a lot of her energy. If she was not careful, she and her boyfriend could drift apart. She could get so worn out that all she wanted to do when she came home was lie on the couch and watch television. Through self-awareness and self-discipline, she prioritized her health and relationship. She made effective choices that created an intentional schedule. While away and at home, she made plans to work out most mornings. She watched her diet while traveling. It was easy to slip into giant heavy meals at restaurants while on the road but she knew all that excessive eating would only further deplete her energy and add to her midsection. She and her boyfriend spoke on the phone often when she was gone. When home, she spent as much time as possible with him, while still maintaining her home, getting good rest and occasionally meeting with friends. This client was not an introvert, so the energy and socializing were possibly easier to manage but she still had to be aware of her priorities, be dependable, and be proactive and intentional for the relationship to thrive during her absences.

WE FIND LOVE IN RELATIONSHIPS?

Couple therapist Bruce Muzik and Dr. Stan Tatkin disagree with the notion we have to love ourselves first. Dr. Tatkin brings up the argument about babies not loving themselves first. They receive love from their parents and learn to love others through this experience. Tatkin also states in *Wired for Love* that chances are if you believe in yourself or "love" yourself it is because someone loved you in the past. The nurturing in past relationships shapes who you are today. A big part of our loving ability is based on how we were loved, and not on how much we love ourselves.

Subsequent chapters will help us decide for ourselves, which comes first: self-love or love.

SYNERGY

The relationship partners have with each other serves as a catalyst to growth and productivity and as a unifying element. Relationships and their synergy create possibilities that were not there. The synergy and interdependence found in mature relationships bring creative cooperation. One plus one can equal eight or eight thousand. The whole is greater than the sum of its parts.

How to achieve synergy? It requires an appreciation for differences, openness to new possibilities, personal security, and a fair amount of vulnerability and courage.

If we have not experienced a lot of synergy or magic of collaboration in our lives, we tend to remain defensive and closed to it. We fear being too vulnerable and subsequently walked over. A nurturing space to grow, make mistakes, sample different methods and admit weaknesses, fosters synergy. Within such a space, we safely learn independence and eventually interdependence.

I mentioned earlier an intuitive writing class I took at a local literary center. The instructor, Roxanne, made it abundantly clear the classroom was a safe place to write and share. There would be no harsh red-pen critiquing or any critical judging of content. We could choose whether or not to read our writing out loud or keep it private. One of the first writers to read her work out loud was an older woman who bravely read of the incarceration of her oldest son. She wrote of the shame but also of the enduring love she felt for him. Her vulnerable words made it easy to empathize with her and her son. After her reading, the floodgates opened. Everyone read his or her work out loud, despite the option to keep silent. The camaraderie and trust level in the room skyrocketed. Suddenly, the classroom and its inhabitants had so much to say. Ideas and memories abounded. The air seemed to crackle with creativity, hope, and joy. Even if the stories were sad, the connection and unity compensated for the sorrow. Individual authenticity caused a tidal wave of relatedness and understanding. It was moving and inspiring to be a part of something so meaningful.

A combination of high trust, openness to new possibilities, and an interest in understanding versus dominating, provides the perfect environment for a synergistic relationship, one where the sum of the parts is greater than the whole. In this setting, the relationship or how each person relates to the other is its own entity and can lead to incredible creative collaboration.

One important point to make is that agreeing all the time or practicing conformity within relationships does not equal unity or oneness. It actually stifles it. Differences are meant to enhance and enrich relationships. To keep each other restrained in our feelings and creativity only serves to devolve our output and collaboration. If we are maturely independent and have self-respect, self-discipline, and self-awareness, then we can handle the risk of disapproval that comes with vulnerability. In effect, we have to have wholeness within ourselves in order to have wholeness in a relationship. It is necessary to dip into the valley of humility to quiet our ego and listen to what others have to contribute that might complement our strengths or weaknesses. We must be able to rely on ourselves and reach out to our partners as well. Independence and interdependence.

CHALLENGES OF GETTING BEYOND INDEPENDENCE AND INTO INTERDEPENDENCE

Our culture loves the independent spirit and the independent person. We value the ability to take care of ourselves. There is a ubiquitous message that permeates society saying, "Don't be needy."

Action steps for sidestepping the independence ideal:

1. Increase your time within nurturing relationships. Nurturing relationships offer love, care and help. They make it safe to depend on others. Mature people understand the ebb and flow of independence and dependency. Search for these people in places that make you feel at ease and alive.

2. Decrease time with people who denigrate you for asking for assistance. If you are secure and mature enough, strive to move them out of their isolation and defensiveness into connection and understanding by showing a willingness to appreciate differences, new possibilities and vulnerability.

3. Take note of all the research pointing to healthier and happier people with robust and loving social lives.

4. Read *Wired for Dating* or *Wired for Love* by Dr. Stan Tatkin to learn about the benefits of a healthy, dependent couple bubble.

Another challenge is loving ourselves first before we can love another.

Action steps for loving yourself so you can give to another person:

1. Know yourself. Practice paying attention, spending time in solitude and with significant others who mirror your good and bad traits. Figure out your values and let them guide you and keep you focused.

2. Like yourself. Gain self-respect by proactively applying self-discipline. Hold yourself responsible by starting a new fitness program or a new job. Start small, wash dishes every day.

3. Become whole. Intentionally work on skills or preferences that challenge you. If you are intensely logical, for example, try following your gut or your heart next time a decision must be made.

4. It is possible to be in a loving relationship while you learn self-discipline and self-respect, but the difficult times in the relationship will be extra challenging due to your budding independence and lack of self-mastery. Seek a partner who desires a committed, growth-fostering relationship. They will make your concerns their concerns and offer support and relief when they see you are stressed.

One other challenge of moving past independence is counteracting a strong counter-dependent reaction.

Action steps for counteracting counter-dependence:

1. Recall whether your parents instilled a strong need to be self-reliant. Did you fend for yourself as a child? Was either of your primary caregivers absent often? Awareness is a start to healing.

2. In small increments, increase the level of intimacy and dependency you feel for a significant other. Instead of running to the store yourself for an ingredient you need for dinner, take your spouse up on their offer to pick it up on their way home. Send a few more texts and maintain eye contact a little longer than you find comfortable.

3. Take note if others say you are aloof and unemotional. Notice the behavior that preceded the remark. Do it less.

Practice Five: Learning from Conflict
Principles of Growth and Healing

"The aim of argument, or of discussion, should not be victory, but progress."—**Joseph Joubert**

There was a lot of conflict between my sister and me growing up. We knew each other's Achilles heels and we used them. We had different temperaments and everyone pointed that out. She was the brash, confident, cute one. I was the quiet, feminine, sweet one. Our differences, instead of being appreciated, became points of competition—a constant subversive question of which temperament was better. Who was the victor? Despite being the older sister, I often felt like the lesser in my parents' eyes and even in my own eyes.

My sister and I fought over everything from the front seat of the car to time in the bathroom. We did not create a safe loving place for each other. There was no progress or resolution or collaboration. I was happy to be out of the house with my friends or tucked up in my room away from the conflict.

Science has proven we choose mates who are familiar or even familial in nature. They remind us of past relationships. I want to emphasize that familiar does not necessarily mean positive. We've all heard stories of people who choose addicted or abusive mates who are just like their parents.

My ex-husband had the conviction, drive and aggressiveness of my sister. It was nice to have someone like him (her) on my team. He was in my corner. He could fight the dragons for me. He could shore me up where I was weak.

We were a good team until the sunshine went away. When I got overwhelmed and felt used and he got stressed and felt used, we became competitors. We both needed love and understanding but instead we competed for appreciation and respect. Ironically, we fell apart when we had financial security and a Christmas-card-perfect home and family.

We did not fight outwardly. We suffered inwardly. We thought we were good parents and spouses because we did not fight. We kept the peace by giving up pieces of ourselves. We did not express ourselves openly. We harbored resentment. It became hard to be around each other because there was so much emotional subterfuge and suppression. We did not feel emotionally safe around each other. It was hard to connect.

According to research reported in the *Journal of Consulting and Clinical Psychology*, couples that address and resolve their conflicts are significantly more satisfied with their relationships than couples that do not.

In truth, we fight because we care. We believe there is something worth fighting for. Only in recent years have I learned to see conflict as two people figuring out a way to move forward together. And I can only do that on my best days, when I am not triggered by fear.

We must all learn a vocabulary to articulate what we want in order to work through dissonance. We learn this by going through phases in our relationship that challenge us. Some call them post-honeymoon, gridlock, or power struggle phases. I call them Reality Phases. They are when we get real and find out if our loved one can and will stand with us.

Reality Phases, where a couple is challenged and forced to work through an obstacle, can happen throughout the lifetime of a relationship, but occur less frequently once a couple has worked through obstacles together and gained maturity and understanding. Reality Phases occur after a Honeymoon Phase and once worked through, lead to more and more secure relationships. Below are the different stages experienced as a couple moves through the relationship maturity continuum.

1. **Honeymoon Phase.** Most of us are familiar with this heady, effortless, dewy-eyed stage. We are on our best behavior and we only see the best qualities in each other. We want to be together all the time.

   There is an attraction fueled by biology and an intoxicating mix of brain chemicals. We are literally high on the feeling of being together. Estrogen and testosterone play a part in initial physical attraction. Interestingly, studies show testosterone drops in men when they are falling in love and rises in women. Both go back to the levels prior to falling in love, after a year or two. Dopamine levels rise when we feel good. It surges on a positive first date. It allows us to sleep and eat less. The more dopamine produced in our body, the more we want it.

It is quite like a chemical addiction. Noradrenaline comes on board and makes our heart race and our palms sweat during new love. We feel energized and anxious, and we are very attentive. The more time we spend with a mate the less noradrenaline is produced, which makes us less scared but also less attentive. Another interesting neurochemical fact is that serotonin (a neurotransmitter that affects mood, appetite, sleep, memory, sexual attraction, and social behavior) drops when we are in love, which makes us obsess about a person more. After a year or two of being in love, serotonin levels should return to normal. This mix of chemicals affects our behavior and our decision-making. It behooves us to know how "out of control" we truly are. Our neurobiology has a big influence.

According to couples therapist Bruce Muzik, the romance or honeymoon stage can last anywhere from two months to two years. What causes it to end? The brain cocktail dissipates and the relationship develops a sense of permanence.

2. Reality Phase. Once one or both partners perceive permanence in the relationship, the struggle kicks in. This is when most couples break up. This is where conflict begins— both internal and external. We realize we have given up parts of ourselves for connection and want ourselves back. Often at this point, we break up and each go on serial dating, always breaking up after the honeymoon phase, or we agree to silently compromise and sacrifice our authenticity and what we really want, to keep the relationship going. If we do the latter, the relationship and we die emotionally. Partners grow apart and unsurprisingly; our sex life suffers.

Elements of automation and attachment surface during this stage. We will discuss attachment theory later in this chapter, but I will address automation now. Neuroscience says our brains constantly look to simplify and automate processes to make less work. Think about when you start a new job. At first, it seems there is a lot to learn and our brains get a workout paying attention to every detail. Over time, some parts of our job become second nature and we move through them with minimal effort. Our relationships and our partners are no different. After a while with our mate, we think we can predict their behavior, so we do not have to be as attentive. We go on autopilot and send fewer texts, make less eye contact and use past experiences to forecast present ones. Our partner feels less seen, heard, and loved and usually lets us know.

What can we do to avoid these outcomes?

Love and fight consciously. Maintain attentiveness and presence. Do not go on autopilot. Stay attuned to our partner. Use the conflict to grow and heal, make progress. Work through arguments until we both feel understood.

Imagine you and your mate have been together over a year. You've fallen into a habit of watching movies together on the weekend; each of you with your phone or iPad in your lap as you sit side-by-side on the couch. The movie plays on the television. Your eyes rarely meet and your attention is directed more at technology than at each other.

To keep love and interest alive, eliminate the extra technology in your laps. Sit closer together and hold hands. Enjoy the movie together. When something funny happens look at your partner and share the humor. If something sad or meaningful happens, again, amplify the moment by looking into your mate's eyes.

Here is another example demonstrating conscious attention over autopilot. A couple that has been together for six months gets in an argument over how much time they spend together. The girlfriend thinks her boyfriend spends too much time with his friends and family and not enough time with her. The boyfriend feels he is considerate of his girlfriend's feelings and that she is overreacting. It would be easy for Girlfriend to go on autopilot and let her experience with a past boyfriend, who often stood her up, shade her perception of her current boyfriend's behavior. That old fear of abandonment speaks loudly in her subconscious. Instead she realizes she is sensitive to distancing behavior and thinks about how important her boyfriend's friends and family are to him. She also remembers how often he invites her to join them in their activities. She quickly acknowledges her fears to her boyfriend and gives him the benefit of the doubt. He suggests doing something, just the two of them, that night.

It should be noted the Reality phase cannot be skipped. Every couple on their way to a secure relationship passes through this struggle. This is when we learn to articulate our needs and generate empathy.

3. The Secure Phase. Once we make it through a Reality Phase, connectedness returns. We learn to accept our partner for who they are. We don't try to change them. There is a sense of respect and security. We stick up for each other and believe and act like we are a team. If one of us hurts the other, we quickly repair any damage we caused. Our partner's concerns are our concerns.

4. The World Bliss Phase. This is the Secure Phase plus the ability to work together to make the world a better place. Together we can do far more than we could alone. There is the synergy mentioned in Practice Four where one plus one equals three or more. We move beyond our intimate relationship into the world. We act as a team and a force for positive change.

FIGHTING IS HEALTHY

Remember, we fight because we care. We want to make our relationship work. To get to the fulfilling Secure and World Bliss stages, we have to fight our way through the Reality Phase. How do we fight consciously? What does it look like when we don't?

Let's start with unproductive fighting, the kind that does not heal or resolve anything. It often starts with an event that sets one or both of us on edge. We may be triggered internally by nuances or memories that remind us of past problems within this relationship or other relationships. Because of the triggering, we disconnect or distance ourselves from our partner emotionally and/or physically. This leads to an argument, which leads to reactive behavior caused by our primitive brain's perceived threat. Reactive behavior could be anything from yelling and swearing to ultimatums to complete withdrawal to multiple "check in" texts throughout the day. The point is it is unproductive and usually leads to more distancing.

Triggering event ⟶ Distancing ⟶ Reactive Behavior ⟶ More Disconnection

Conscious or attentive fighting is productive. It starts out the same with an inciting event and disconnection from our partner, but it moves into the type of arguing that aims for clarity and understanding. The goal is to work together until we each feel heard and understood. This kind of fighting involves empathy and responsiveness, subjects we will go deep into in the next chapter, but for now responsiveness means listening to our partner's requests for attention and responding to them without clouding our reaction with our own autobiography or defensiveness. Once we achieve a feeling of being understood, we reconnect. Our intimacy improves and we move out of the Reality Phase.

Triggering event $\longrightarrow$ Distancing $\longrightarrow$ Attentive Behavior $\longrightarrow$
Reconnection

An important point to remember is that every complaint or issue our partner or we bring up has a fear and a need for connection behind it. No one truly likes being disconnected. Not even introverts. As we said in the previous chapter, humans are social creatures wired for love and interacting.

Think of a consistent issue you have with your mate. It could be something like, "He is often negative and judgmental." Now think of the worry behind it. What are you afraid of? What is the worst-case scenario you envision? It could be, "I worry he may start being critical and mean to me. I am afraid I won't be able to take that, so I'll withdraw or end the relationship."

Lastly, with your complaint or perceived issue, what are you really asking for? In our example about our negative and judgmental partner, it could be, "I want to feel safe around my partner so I can make mistakes and be vulnerable. I want to relax and be close with him." Does this need remind you of a previous relationship, perhaps with a family member or ex-partner? Often our fears or worries stem from old wounds created when we were children or in a different relationship. All our relationships shape us into the people we are today. They plant the seeds for how we handle closeness and conflict.

*"I am not sure that I exist, actually, I am all the writers that I have read,
all the people that I have met, all the (men) that I have loved;
all the cities I have visited."* —**Jorge Luis Borges**

ATTACHMENT THEORY

Attachment theory tells us that our beliefs and expectations about relationships have their origins in our earliest childhood relationships. The quality of our relationships with our first primary caregivers, affects our future intimate relationships.

If our first relationships were secure, loving, and safe, we have a better chance of experiencing secure, loving relationships in the future. If our parent/child relationships were more insecure, with less emotional stability and protection, then we are at greater risk for forming less stable and insecure relationships in adulthood.

Attachment theory in psychology originated in 1958 with the work of John Bowlby. In the 1930s, John Bowlby worked as a psychiatrist in London, where he treated many emotionally disturbed children.

This experience led Bowlby to consider the importance of the child's relationship with their mother in terms of their social, emotional, and cognitive development. It shaped his belief about the link between early infant separation from the mother and later maladjustment. This led Bowlby to formulate his attachment theory.

Bowlby, working alongside James Robertson in 1952 observed that children experienced intense distress when separated from their mothers. Even when other caregivers fed the children, their distress did not diminish. Hence, the anxiety was not simply hunger or a desire for food. They missed the connection with their mother.

Bowlby later defined attachment as a "lasting psychological connectedness between human beings."

Psychologist Mary Ainsworth later (1971 and 1978) designed and carried out a study called The Strange Situation. Infants one to two years old were put into a child-friendly setting with their mother and a stranger. At different times throughout the experiment the child was either with his or her mother alone in the toy-filled room, with his or her mother and the stranger in the room, alone with the stranger in the room or alone in the room. The psychologists then observed the infants' reaction to each setting.

Insecurely and securely attached children reacted very differently to the absence and return of their mothers.

Securely attached children were confident in their caregiver's ability to soothe them if they were upset. They safely explored the room when their parent was present and became distressed when they left. They were quickly soothed when their mother returned.

The study concluded children develop a sense of security when their caregiver is sensitive to their needs and responds to them competently. Securely attached children made up the majority of the children in Mary Ainsworth's studies.

Infants with an insecurely avoidant attachment style did not orient to their caregiver when exploring the room. They did not seek their mother when they were distressed. They were very independent of their caregiver emotionally and physically. Ainsworth concluded that these caregivers were insensitive and even rejecting of their child's needs. In times of distress this parent was often unavailable. Because the parent did not value closeness, the child stopped seeking it and may have even started viewing it as intrusive. Insecure avoidant children made up about 15% of the children in the study.

Insecurely ambivalent children exhibited clingy or dependent behavior with their mother and were hesitant to leave her and explore the room. They were not soothed by their mother and often rejected her interactions. The child did not have a developed sense of security from the caregiver. They were ambivalent about closeness, both wanting it and rejecting it. This behavior was concluded to be the result of inconsistent responsiveness (close and attentive sometimes, unavailable other times) from the mother. These children also made up 15% of Ainsworth's studies.

Attachment theory is not limited to the infancy stage of life. The child/parent interactions or lack thereof that occur beyond infancy (into childhood, adolescence and adulthood) affect our tolerance for intimacy and relationships as well. Relationships we form as adults also mold our ability to form secure bonds.

Our brains have plasticity. Neural pathways grow and change with repetition of positive or negative interactions. We can move from being insecurely attached as young children to more securely attached as adults—all based on the relationships we form along the way.

ALTERNATE ATTACHMENT THEORY

An alternate attachment theory proposed in 1984 by Jerome Kagan suggested the temperament of the child is what leads to different attachment types. Children with different innate temperaments will have different attachment types. Research in 1989 found babies with an "easy" temperament (eat and sleep regularly, accepting of new experiences) are likely to develop secure attachments. Babies who were "slow to warm up" and took a while to get used to new experiences are likely to have insecure avoidant attachments. Babies with a "difficult" temperament who eat and sleep irregularly and reject new experiences are likely to have insecure ambivalent attachments.

INNATE TEMPERAMENT THEORY AND INTROVERSION / HIGH SENSITIVITY

The innate temperament theory made me wonder about the correlation between introversion, high sensitivity, and attachment. Many highly sensitive people are introverts. High sensitivity in infants could mean fussy, slow to warm up, and not easily consoled, hence a more insecure attachment with their primary caregiver.

The most complete explanation of why children develop different attachment types could be an interactionist theory. In other words, attachment type is a result of a combination of the child's innate temperament and their parents' sensitivity toward their needs.

WHY ATTACHMENT THEORY IS IMPORTANT TO RELATIONSHIPS

As mentioned earlier, it has been shown that our attachment style affects how we handle closeness as adults. It offers an explanation of why we react to closeness and intimacy with ease or discomfort. It gives us valuable information about why we may distance ourselves or cling to a partner. It helps us explain the discomfort we feel or the conflict we create with a significant other.

If we understand our attachment style we can connect with our partner better and heal wounds from our past primary relationships. We can fight consciously and productively, versus using our primitive brain and reacting subconsciously and unproductively.

As mentioned, it is possible to move toward secure attachment with an intimate partner as an adult. We change depending upon our current primary relationship. Ideally, we maintain secure attachment or move along the continuum to achieve it. Insecurely avoidant attachment style is the least secure, ambivalent is next, and of course, securely attached is the most secure.

It should be noted that attachment styles are not mental disorders or indicators of our mental health, nor is it bad to be insecurely attached. Dr. Tatkin says more than 50% of people are securely attached, leaving less than 50% insecurely attached.

Knowing our attachment style gives us an edge when starting or maintaining a relationship. The first step to a mature, secure relationship is knowing who we are, knowing what we bring to the table. For true interdependence, we strive to be authentic within a relationship. We know and honor ourselves while knowing and honoring our partner and the relationship.

Whether each person is securely or insecurely attached is not the most important factor, what matters most is the willingness of both partners to work toward and sustain a secure functioning relationship.

SECURE ATTACHMENT IN ADULTHOOD

The secure foundation provided in childhood, where their physical and emotional needs were sensitively met, allows these children to grow up to be adults who form satisfying relationships. Their lives make sense to them. They understand that hardships they've experienced (childhood trauma, failures, relationship disasters, disease, or any kind of emotional pain) are parts of a larger, more comprehensive and positive life story. They tend to be empathic, concerned, and patient with family and other people. They're good listeners. They make friends more easily and can take on professional challenges better than insecurely attached adults. They're more likely to appreciate and cherish their children for who they are, rather than who they want them to be. They seem happy most of the time.

In a love relationship, they work together well and see their partner as a safe space, and their partner feels the same about them. They make their partner's concerns their concerns. They know two is better than one.

Securely attached adults are affectionate, emotionally and physically engaging, and not afraid to be themselves. They strive to be sensitive to their partner. When in disagreement, they work to come up with a win/win solution. They are not afraid of engulfment or abandonment. They are collaborators. They are resilient with a stability that stems from their ability to depend on others. This resilience and stability gives them the courage to move toward self-improvement. They have a willingness to learn and grow.

Here is a personal example to show the difference between a secure partner and an insecure one. I went on dates with two different men to the same restaurant. On date number one with a man I had dated for over a year, we were seated near the bar. It was quite noisy there. I wanted to enjoy an intimate meal with my boyfriend and I worried the bar noise would interfere with my focus. As I've mentioned, I have a highly sensitive nervous system. When I voiced my thoughts about the loudness of the bar and possibly moving tables, my boyfriend got agitated. Between gritted teeth he asked, "What do you want to do Brenda?" I could tell he was annoyed, so I decided to not make waves and live with the background noise.

On date number two with someone I had been seeing for eight months, we were seated by the window where two heat vents blasted extremely warm air right on us. I said something about it being very warm at our table. I wondered out loud about switching tables. Date number two agreed it was warm and said, "Should we see if we can move tables or get the wait staff to turn off the vents?" The waiter was more than happy to shut off the vents. We had a lovely intimate dinner.

The second date knew how to make my concerns his concerns. He worked with me to come to a solution we both liked. He did not make me feel small.

AVOIDANT ATTACHMENT IN ADULTHOOD

The lack of attentiveness and availability from their caregiver as children causes avoidantly attached types to learn self-reliance. They essentially take on the role of parenting themselves. They value their independence and like to do their own problem-solving. They do not want to burden anyone with their needs because in their mind, they most likely won't be met anyway, so why risk rejection or disappointment?

They often come off as focused on themselves and may overly attend to their creature comforts.

They have strengths such as the ability to focus on tasks, which helps them excel at their jobs. They tend to be logical and detail oriented. They do not pay attention or address emotions, theirs or others', as much as other attachment styles. Performance and appearance are important to them. They care a lot about what others think. They spend a lot of time on internal processes, so they can be deep thinkers. They do not like personal conflict and so are ready to compromise or negotiate.

Close relationships tend to be more stressful for the avoidantly attached person. People with an avoidant attachment tend to lead more inward lives, both denying the importance of loved ones and detaching easily from them. They are often defensive and have the ability to shut down emotionally.

When they were young they learned to comfort themselves, and self-regulate. They became good at entertaining themselves. As adults, it can be a relief to get away from others, particularly when they are stressed. Sound familiar introverts? They find it easier to regulate their own nervous system. A clingy partner is especially threatening to an avoidant person. The "needy" partner represents a part of themselves they are ashamed of and they threaten an avoidant individual's self-regulating alone time.

They may exhibit distancing behavior such as withdrawing, criticizing, working all the time, flirting with others, and telling their partner they are too needy to avoid getting too close to someone.

Despite appearing to desire independence, the avoidant individual still wants connection and affection. They want to get past their fear of rejection or unavailability from their partner (like their caregiver in childhood) and work toward a secure relationship.

AMBIVALENT ATTACHMENT IN ADULTHOOD

An ambivalently attached adult's biggest fear is being abandoned, punished, or rejected. They're frequently looking to their partner to rescue or complete them. Although they're seeking a sense of safety and security by clinging to their partner, their actions push their partner away.

Ambivalent partners focus on meaning, relationships and emotions. They tend to be sensitive and often are involved in the arts or counseling fields. They talk in a non-linear fashion, which can drive the more logical, and rational person crazy. Ambivalent adults like to connect through touch and talk. They relax and are happiest with others. They tend to be more expressive verbally and physically. When under stress they move toward others versus away (as the insecure avoidant person does). They did not learn how to regulate their own emotions so rely on others to help them and give them cues how to do it. For these reasons, they can be seen as clingy.

They are affectionate and can be generous, caring and giving, sometimes at the sacrifice of their own needs. Trouble arises when they do not feel the same in return. Resentment surfaces and old wounds from childhood reopen. They may exhibit anger and even withdraw like the avoidantly attached, although the ambivalent person often subconsciously does it in the hope that a partner will seek them out or chase them. The insecure ambivalent person ultimately desperately wants love and companionship.

To picture an ambivalently attached person in action, imagine a young couple on a date at a restaurant. Susie asks her date, Vanessa, what she was like as a teenager. Vanessa compliments Susie on her great question and then rattles on for five minutes about everything from her hairstyle as a teen to her relationship with her mom. Then at the end of her reply she apologizes for oversharing. She really likes Susie and wants the relationship to work but now worries she might have been too talkative. She reaches out to take Susie's hand. Susie, who is a secure partner, takes Vanessa's hand in hers, looks her in the eyes and reassures her she loved hearing more about her childhood. Vanessa, who has an ambivalent attachment style, relaxes and hopes Susie asks her out again.

AVOIDANTS, AMBIVALENTS, INTROVERTS, AND EXTROVERTS

Do insecurely avoidant and insecurely ambivalent types sound a bit like introverts and extroverts respectively? The insecurely avoidant type definitely exhibits behavior similar to sensitive introverts, with their need to self-regulate and distance themselves from others.

I began to question whether we are products of our families of origin or of our innate temperament. Perhaps like the interactionist theory proposed regarding attachment styles, we are a combination of both.

ATTACHMENT STYLES SURFACE DURING THE REALITY PHASE

Once we perceive a relationship to have permanence, we project old attachment injuries/memories onto our partner. The nature of intimate relationships—consistent time together, loving and depending on someone—reminds us of our earliest relationships and creates more opportunity for discord. The need for authenticity struggles to balance with the need for companionship. Each attachment style has a different way of dealing with conflict within a relationship.

CONFLICT AND RELIEF FOR THE SECURELY ATTACHED

Just because someone has a secure attachment style does not mean his or her relationships are conflict-free. All relationships have disagreements. As I said earlier, every couple goes through the Reality stage. This is when authenticity arises and contrasts with our partner's understandably different perspective. Using the maturity definition, we found from Stephen Covey, we must have courage and consideration to resolve conflict. Securely attached individuals have an easier time with this. They are mature enough to courageously express themselves honestly and considerate enough to care how their message impacts their partner.

Given their secure childhood foundation, they trust that their partner has good intentions and do not let dissonance ruffle them. They look for mutually positive ways to work through conflict with their partner. They know themselves and have enough self-respect and resilience to weather obstacles in the relationship. That said, if a partner does not have enough of the same commitment and willingness to work toward win/win solutions and growth, a secure person may move on to someone who does. They expect to be treated well. They intend to treat their significant other well. If they make a mistake they repair it quickly. They do not regularly distance or cling. They bring stability to relationships.

CONFLICT AND RELIEF FOR THE INSECURELY AVOIDANT ATTACHMENT TYPE

Because avoidant types learned to self-regulate, self-soothe, and self-stimulate in childhood, close relationships tend to be more difficult for them. They quite often find themselves with ambivalent partners, possibly because the initial rush of warmth and affection from the ambivalent person is so pleasing and reassuring. Also, it could be the familiarity of an insecure attachment that attracts them. As mentioned earlier, familiar and familial traits attract us. Either way, the avoidant's self-care can upset and cause conflict with a partner who expects and desires engagement (which both securely attached and ambivalently attached people desire). Especially when under stress, an avoidant type tends to withdraw from their people in order to find relief. This is distancing behavior and may look like the following: less eye contact, focusing on technology, spending a lot of time alone, or talking about themselves without listening. There are many ways distancing behavior exhibits itself. These are just a few examples. Threats to autonomy are scary for someone with an insecure avoidant attachment style. Depending on someone else leaves him or her vulnerable.

The avoidant type fears rejection, unavailability, and pain. Their primary caregiver was not there for them or was not there in a positive way. Distancing protects them. They subconsciously reject before being rejected.

How to resolve conflict with an avoidantly attached partner?

To move toward a secure relationship a partner needs to understand the shame the avoidant type feels about dependency. He or she was not allowed such dependency as a child. They learned self-reliance and independence were more valuable and expected than care and dependency.

The insecurely avoidant partner appreciates praise, reassurance and constructive feedback. A loving partner must not take distancing behavior personally and remain patient and steadfastly by his or her side. A secure partner can raise an insecure partner's security status. This is not to say a secure person should accept poor treatment or neglect from a partner. If there is no willingness from the avoidantly attached partner to move toward their partner, then the relationship will not last. If a secure partner consistently demonstrates acceptance, understanding, and openness and grants an avoidant partner space, and the avoidant type does not gradually move toward closeness with them, it may be wise to seek a more available partner.

CONFLICT RELIEF FOR THE INSECURELY AMBIVALENT ATTACHMENT TYPE

The relationship-focused and giving nature of the ambivalent type means they truly want to be with another person. Unfortunately, sometimes their deep desire for engagement and emotional connection makes them seem high maintenance and clingy to their partner, particularly an avoidant type. This causes friction.

An ambivalent type's lack of ability to manage themselves, makes it difficult to form interdependent relationships. There is too much dependency on the other person's emotions, needs, interactions and approval. When the ambivalent person believes, their significant other is not coming through for them, they react unproductively. They may withdraw or create distance as the avoidant person does, but it is often just a tactic to get the other person to feel bad and check on them. They may also drive their partner crazy with constant pleas for attention such as countless texts throughout the day, all with a subtext of "Do you love me?" Ambivalents like to take the temperature of the relationship all the time, constantly looking for perceived threats. They want proof they are wanted and cared for, like the proof they work to provide for their partner. Proof helps their fear of abandonment subside, for a while. Ironically, if they feel slighted or that the relationship is threatened, they may express anger, push their lover away, hurt their lover's feelings, get emotional, and leave their partner confused and feeling abandoned.

To avoid such an outcome the ambivalently attached person needs to learn how to manage their emotions and communicate earnestly and directly. They need to learn how to get their message across without putting their partner on the defensive. Ambivalents are known for giving hints and beating around the bush when it comes to getting what they really want. Taking charge of their words, emotions and actions goes a long way toward creating an interdependent relationship.

Their partner can help them become more self-reliant by reassuring them often that they are loved and cared for. This can be done verbally or preferably by responding consistently with affirming actions. For example, if you make a plan to meet on Saturday at 6:00 p.m., then show up on time and hold his or her hand throughout the night. This will relieve the ambivalently attached person's nervous system. Ambivalent types love calming and affectionate gestures. They allow them to relax and stop taking the temperature of the relationship.

WE HAVE TRAITS OF DIFFERENT ATTACHMENT STYLES

We all have tendencies from each of the attachment styles. We may be avoidant in some situations and more ambivalent in others, and at still other times we may exhibit secure behavior. Just like introversion and extroversion, we are somewhere on the spectrum of each attachment style. Usually, one is slightly more dominant. We are not purely one type.

Spending time in secure relationships with therapists, friends, family, and lovers can also help us move from a dominantly insecure attachment style to a secure one.

I have tendencies from all three attachment styles. The close relationships I have had, gave me experience in all three types. As a child, there was an avoidant (me) and ambivalent (sister) dynamic between my sister and me. I withdrew from her in order to self-soothe and get away from her constant criticism. She would pursue me, always hoping for a companion, but then "punishing" me with harsh words when I did play with her. My father had avoidant tendencies and my mother was ambivalent. I had a grandmother, who visited every couple of months, who provided security.

As an adult, the relationship with my dad became more secure. In my marriage, I ended up showing avoidant traits to my husband's secure/avoidant style. Over the years and after more relationship experience, I have moved toward more secure traits mixed with ambivalence and avoidance. For example, I suffer feelings of abandonment (ambivalent) when my partner is not available regularly or changes plans at the last minute to be with friends rather than me, but also find myself asking for time to work or just be by myself often enough to seem avoidant. I expect fair and just treatment from my partner and strive to provide attentive responsiveness to him while respecting my authenticity, which demonstrates my more secure side.

Knowledge and understanding of each type helps me guide my coaching clients to clarity and growth in their relationships.

An important point I want to emphasize is that our close relationships (including ones with therapists or coaches) can heal us from the old wounds created in childhood or in previous adult relationships. Our close people will not only be the ones triggering our attachment styles, they will be the ones helping us work through them. Again, it takes a willingness to grow and work toward a secure relationship to invoke healing and maturity. A partner, who challenges us but also reassures and supports us, transforms our relationship and us.

OWNING OUR CONTRIBUTION TO THE CONFLICT

To move forward in our career, relationships and personal development, we have to learn how to resolve conflict and own our contribution to it.

> *"It is only through a vast amount of experience and a lengthy and successful maturation process that we gain the capacity to see the world and our place in it realistically, and thus are enabled to realistically assess our responsibility for ourselves and the world."* —Dr. M. Scott Peck, *The Road Less Traveled*

AUTHENTICITY INVITES CONFRONTATION

To be truly authentic, I've found I have to learn how to express my feelings and ideas. I have to outwardly share my inner world. This sometimes causes discord with others. They don't have the same priorities or values. They feel hurt, annoyed or frustrated by my words and ways.

Many of you understand how uncomfortable disagreement is to a deeply feeling and harmony-loving person. We make our decisions based on feelings—our own and those of others. Leaving ourselves wide open to criticism or judgment is nerve-wracking. When under stress, we operate from pure emotion. Discord has us scrambling to return the peace to avoid personal outbursts and pain to others and ourselves.

My heart skips a beat every time someone disagrees with something I write, but yet, I can't stop telling my story. I have this strong desire to connect with and help others. That desire and yes, the positive responses I receive, overpower the fear.

SELF-CONFRONTING, WE HAVE TO DO IT

It took me a while to fully own up to my contribution to the breakdown of my marriage. I put the majority of the blame for our divorce on my ex-husband. It was four years after our divorce before I could I say I didn't work hard enough to understand/ accept/love him.

When we were married, I talked contemptuously about him with my friends and family. I didn't have his back.

I was not open to fostering his growth unless he understood and supported mine.

I wanted to stay true to myself but not within the relationship.

WE ARE RESPONSIBLE FOR OUR HAPPINESS AND THE HEALTH OF OUR RELATIONSHIP

Two major things I have learned through subsequent relationships, thousands of hours of research, and countless hours of self-examination, are: 1) To acknowledge my contribution to the conflict in a relationship; and 2) To work toward resolution with my partner. I can't just plan to change my partner or change the relationship. I have to be open to changing me. If we don't take responsibility for our contribution to the argument and its resolution, then relief is solely in the hands of the other person. We remain steadfastly in victimhood. If we take ownership we self-direct and lead our lives.

One of my favorite phrases my significant other uses is, "We'll figure this out." When we come to a crossroads or conflict in our relationship, he'll reassure me with those words. I now find myself using them with him. I also like, "How can I help?" Both sentences lead to mutual resolution of the issue.

CONFESSION

I didn't try very hard to teach my husband what being an introvert and highly sensitive person meant. I was still embarrassed by it. I was empty and anxious and it seemed he just expected me to keep barreling through life. I was so worn out. I wanted to be understood and supported emotionally.

His presence usually meant putting on my dynamic-mom mask because he had such drive and intensity. He thrived on the meritocratic lifestyle. I withered. I wanted to love him, but I didn't really know him. I only knew the way of living he provided and embodied. That turned me off.

Admittedly, I spent little time trying to figure out what his fears were. He never showed much emotion other than occasional anger. I never felt a sense of safety and warmth. I assumed he was incapable of deep emotions and true connection.

I felt shame and guilt for needing time away from my family. I didn't know how to own my way of being, show up consistently for others, or earn respect. I asked for freedom. I was cold. I was lonely. Like an avoidantly attached person, I withdrew. I found validation and understanding from others (like an ambivalent type). I caused a lot of hurt.

According to the article, "The Art of Confrontation: How Conflict Can Improve a Feeler's Relationships", research from Baylor University's College of Arts and Sciences found withdrawal is far more prevalent in distressed relationships and has a negative impact on a couple's ability to resolve an issue.

I SEE YOU AND WANT TO UNDERSTAND YOU

Understanding the other person's point of view and expressing our understanding back to them go a long way toward conflict resolution. When we are at odds with a partner, friend, or family member, our knee-jerk reaction is to stand up for ourselves. We want to relay our needs or wants and have the other person accommodate us. They have to change in order for us to be happy. Quite often if we get perspective, we figure out it is us who need to change. Antonia Dodge of the personality typing website and podcast Personality Hacker says that personal growth is when we slap our foreheads and say, "Oh! I'm the asshole!"

How many times have we fought with someone to no avail? There was no resolution, just back and forth defensiveness. Defensiveness means the other person does not feel heard or understood. They still want to plead their case. The secret to stopping the defensive, unproductive spiral is to stop replying with our own points and wants and to start replying to our partner's points and wants. Shift from our perspective to theirs. Ask questions about their point of view until they feel understood. We say things like, "Let me see if I have this right. You are upset because I spent too much time looking at my phone at dinner and that made you feel unimportant?" We rephrase what they said, to show we are listening. When we have a good grasp on our partner's perspective, we can say, "That makes sense that you feel that way because I would feel ignored too if you looked at your phone all night." Relationship therapist, Jayson Gaddis, teaches the comforting effect of the phrase, "That makes sense." When we hear it, we feel like our partner is tuned into us. It's both validating and empathic.

We know our partner feels heard because we ask, "Is there anything else you would like to say?" until they say, "No." If we are in a loving secure relationship, our partner will do the same for us. Once armed with clarity, win/win solutions are within reach.

WIN/LOSE

The competitive, résumé virtue laden meritocracy we live in often has us existing in a win/lose or lose/win environment. If we are immersed in a world of conditional love, where we have to be better than others or live up to other's expectations (dependency) to receive approval we are set up for a win/lose outcome. This mentality insists there is not enough love, wealth, happiness, etc. to go around. It's often called the scarcity mentality. It leads us to use power, money, and status to get what we want. Those things don't fuel love relationships. They put us on the defensive and diminish creativity and cooperation.

WIN/WIN

Win/win believes in an alternative third response. It is not about you winning or me winning. It's about finding a better way so we both win. It is not the same thing as a compromise. In a compromise, both parties give up a little of their desired outcome so 1 + 1 = 1 ½. Win/win is synergistic, as mentioned in Practice Three, because the whole is greater than the sum of its parts. 1 + 1 = 3 or more. It is the best option for an interdependent relationship because in the long run if it is not a win for both partners, it eventually becomes a loss for both. Repressed resentment or sadness caused by too many losses always surfaces, usually in impulsive, negative, reactive ways. A win/win practice begins with the character of the people involved and includes consideration of the relationship.

Couples in or working toward a secure relationship trust each other. They are mindful of their partner's needs, so distancing and clinging are minimized. With trust as a foundation, they are able to focus on the issues rather than personalities or position. There is enough reassurance and security in the relationship to allow for open communication, learning and creativity—all fertile ground for win/win solutions.

Win/lose is transactional. Win/win is transformational. In win/win, interdependent synergy takes place, transforming the individuals and the relationship.

According to Roger Fisher and William Ury's classic book on negotiating, *Getting to Yes*, there are several key components of a win/win process.

- One is to see the problem from the other person's perspective, to understand their point of view and their desires

- Another is to focus on interests and concerns, not positions

- A third component is to come up with solutions that represent a mutual gain

Here's an example of win/win in action. Adam and Lucy have been married for ten years. They have two young children and busy careers. Lately, they can't find any time for each other. Adam gets up early and goes to work, while Lucy sleeps later and gets the children off to school. Lucy is a night owl and stays up until 11:00 p.m. watching television or working on her laptop, while Adam goes to bed at 9:00 p.m. just after putting the kids down. They both value their relationship and enjoy each other's company. They take care to listen to each other and shore each other up when one needs help. They are a team.

With Adam leaving early and Lucy staying up late, they are like ships in the night, missing out on connecting during one-on-one time.

Adam knows Lucy enjoys her alone time at night. It helps her wind down and come back to herself. Lucy knows Adam has the most energy in the morning and likes to get to work early while it's still quiet at the office.

Adam could force himself to stay up later to spend time with Lucy, but that would be a lose/win for him and for Lucy too, because likes having alone time at night. Lucy could go to bed early or get up early to spend time with Adam, but that would be a sacrifice or lose/win for her. Because they truly respect each other and make their relationship a priority, they put their heads together to come up with a win/win solution.

They came up with a fulfilling option. Instead of watching TV or working on her computer right away after the kids are in bed, Lucy would get ready for bed with Adam and put Adam to bed. They would spend time talking about their days, working through any issues that needed resolving, reading to each other, or making love. After tucking him in, she was free to watch TV or work on her laptop. It looks like a compromise, because both partners give a little time but the result is more than the input. It is not merely transactional, i.e. "I'll trade a little of my time for a little of yours." The small give from each person, lifts their relationship and each of their self-esteem to a new level. It reinforces their trust and gives them the intimacy they crave. They both got what they wanted. They both slept better too because of the oxytocin boost from the physical intimacy and the overall relaxing effect mutuality and security bring.

WHY THE HARD CONVERSATIONS ARE IMPORTANT

Most people do not enjoy conflict, but without it the depth and growth of our relationships suffer.

We could withdraw and avoid disagreements, which, although appealing to introverts and avoidant attachment types, does not allow us to go back and forth getting each other's perspective. It doesn't allow us to mitigate defensiveness or form win/ win solutions. It does not give our partner any reassurance. Withdrawing briefly to get calm and personal clarity is acceptable if a return time is given and our partner is assured of our commitment to work through the issue.

We could avoid all difficult conversations and keep our relationships emotionless and superficially focused, but then there is no vulnerability, growth, or intimacy. The hard conversations and their resolutions are often where the connection, maturity, respect, and trust develop. This tactic could leave us feeling lonely within a relationship.

We could give in every time and let a lose/win dynamic take over, letting losses and resentment pile up until they have to be released in impulsive, unproductive reactions. I think it is clear that is not a good option.

What it comes down to is that conflict is necessary. It gets us back to our integrity and fosters our wholeness. It makes us work on our character and our relationship. The tension it causes is often the catalyst that makes us change, take action, and grow.

Carl Jung said we choose partners to expand who we are. We experience conflict and healing through relationships. Our partners ideally challenge and support us on our path to wholeness.

THE CHALLENGE OF CONFLICT AND ACTION STEPS TO RELIEVE IT

Conflict feels like a challenge to our security, but intentional behavior versus reactive behavior, turns conflict into an opportunity to heal and grow toward wholeness and maturity. The next time there is tension between you and your loved one, apply the following actions to allow the disagreement to transform your relationship from insecure to secure:

1. Do not avoid the conflict. Avoidance only makes it worse.

2. Do not react with your primitive brain. Get calm first. Take deep breaths. Give yourself time to gather yourself but let your partner know when you will return. Name the emotions you feel. Consider whether the friction is related to a wound you suffered in the past.

3. Think about your contribution. Are you projecting the behavior of a past intimate partner onto your current partner? How did you incite this friction? Did you react impulsively, not consciously?

4. Return to your partner and initiate repair swiftly regarding your contribution to the argument. Threats to a relationship tend to expand and invade our hearts and minds quickly and need to be nipped in the bud as soon as possible. Start by meeting face-to-face and touch, hold hands, or hug your partner to let

them know you have good intentions and want to be close with them.

5. Next, ask questions that help you understand your partner's perspective. Rephrase their answers until their reaction makes sense to you and you can tell them so. Do not deny or discount their experience. Listen for clarity and understanding, not to be right or to win. Resist the urge to respond with your own story.

6. Ask them if they have anything else to share, until they don't. If they are defensive, they don't feel completely heard yet.

7. Use your knowledge of their relationship history and attachment style to soothe them. If they are insecurely avoidant, give them space to self-regulate and make sure their worst fears (rejection, unavailability, punishment) do not happen. Reassure them you wish to work this out and stay together. If they are insecurely ambivalent, provide lots of reassurance and make sure their worst fears (abandonment, inconsistent attention) do not come true. Tell them you are in it for the long haul and want to come out stronger as a couple after working through this conflict. Use your knowledge of your own attachment style to head off unproductive reactions. Use words to respectfully ask for space if you are an avoidant type. Manage your emotions and give your partner space to process the situation if you are an ambivalent type. Lean on your own integrity and ability to comfort and depend on someone else to help regain connection with your partner if you are securely attached.

8. Bask in the warmth of conflict resolution. Working through an obstacle moves you further out of the Reality Phase and into the Secure Phase. Trust is earned. It heals old wounds and fosters personal growth.

Practice Six: Calming Each Other's Nervous Systems Principles of Responsiveness

"You're not like the others. I've seen a few; I know. When I talk, you look at me. When I said something about the moon, you looked at the moon, last night." —**Ray Bradbury**

I've known for years that my nervous system is more easily aroused than about 80% of the population. I startle more often. I can only handle groups of people for so long before I need quiet time to myself. I am highly attuned to other's energy—positive or negative. Anything from emotions to lighting can feel overstimulating to me.

I HAVEN'T ALWAYS FELT HIGHLY SENSITIVE

Growing up, I did not generally feel overstimulated. It was not until I found myself married with three children living in the successful suburbs that I started to feel overwhelmed frequently. The materialistic and achievement focused lifestyle hit the tipping point of my ability to manage it in a composed manner.

I often felt alone. During the marriage, and especially toward the end of it, there was not a lot of soothing going on between my husband and me. We both did our best to heal our own wounds and those of our children, but those took us farther away from each other. We did not know how to work through the stress together. We were not capable of supporting each other emotionally, but a lot of emotions—such as anger, sadness, overwhelm—lingered in our home.

AROUSAL AND STRESS

We talked about self-soothing in the independence section of this book. I still believe it is a valuable skill; however, a truth for me is that it is most effective if done within a secure and supportive relationship.

The ability to soothe our partner and vice versa leads to relationship sustainability.

Our nervous system regulates how calm or excited we are at any given moment. This is our state of arousal. Highly sensitive persons live with a naturally higher state of arousal.

Most of the time, our brain and nervous system respond automatically, without a lot of conscious thought, particularly if we are under stress. Our nervous systems are especially wired to notice any threats in our environment. For our survival, threats register stronger in our nervous systems than positive or loving behavior do. Originally, our nervous systems focused on protecting us from dangerous predators, but since we have evolved to the point of minimal danger of being eaten by a tiger, our brains now focus on everyday stress and even our loved ones as potential threats.

Wouldn't it be better if our partners were soothers of our arousal system versus threats to it?

TRIGGERS AND RESPONSES

I've been triggered into over arousal by such things as tone of voice, driving too fast, or too much negativity from a partner. Now those aren't exactly life-threatening (well maybe the fast driving was), but my nervous system reacted as if I'd been physically hurt. My fight-or-flight response kicked in. My heart raced, my mouth dried, I spoke slower, I perspired.

Once in a calmer state of mind, I tried to explain to my partner how the perceived threatening behaviors affected me, but my words triggered him into a defensive state of alert. Instead of soothing each other and helping each other relax, we escalated our threat responses.

What I did not know then, was how to not take my lover's threat reactions personally. I did not understand his responses were wired into him long before me (perhaps from childhood or previous relationships, i.e. attachment issues). I did not recognize his elevated stimulation as an automatic response. It simply felt like danger and discomfort to me. I protected myself instead of working harder to soothe him.

HOW TO SOOTHE OUR PARTNER

The first thing to do is notice when our loved one exhibits a high negative state of arousal (there are positive states such as excitement). Become familiar with the behavior or perceived threats that make our partner's nervous system sound the alarms. Are there experiences from her past that make her uneasy? Does questioning his judgment set your lover off?

If we see our partner begin to struggle—talk in a clipped manner, breathe faster, sweat, fidget, get tongue-tied—move in quickly to help. According to Dr. Tatkin, we perceive threats very quickly and automatic reactions transpire just as fast.

Two ways to soothe our loved one are nonverbal calming and verbal reassurance. Examples of nonverbal calming are reaching out and taking your partner's hand, rubbing their shoulders or giving them a wink across the table when a discussion gets heated. Different people respond better or worse to different methods. A verbal reassurance could be as simple as starting a discussion with "I love you and I want to work this out," or verbally expressing gratitude for something we love about our relationship. It makes sense that the partner who feels most secure at the time sets aside his or her issues and cares for the other.

If we learn how to recognize and regulate our partner's nervous system and do it consistently, we build trust. The future holds fewer and fewer instances of survival mode and knee-jerk reactions.

NURTURING

One way to soothe our partner's nervous system is through nurturing. According to psychotherapist Dr. Webb, nurturance is a combination of love, care, and help. Children and adults kept away from love, care, and help for too long build walls and have a hard time giving and receiving nurturing affection.

In our current climate of merit-based love and success, it is easy for children and adults to feel they are not truly heard or appreciated for who they are, but for their performances and achievements. Physical nurturing (transportation, academic tutoring, food preparation, directing) outweighs emotional nurturing (love, care, help, listening to understand). As competition and conditional love proliferate, the void where warmth and a safe harbor could exist continues to grow.

ONE THING MEN WANT MORE THAN SEX

In his article "The One Thing Men Want More Than Sex", Jed Diamond, PhD writes that a safe harbor where men can feel nurtured is more appealing than the sexual act itself. Always wanting sex is seen as a manly trait and supposedly sorts the alpha males from the beta males—at least in a competitive, performance-based environment. But that competition is a cold business, and according to Diamond, most men want warmth and a safe harbor. They want to be nurtured. Diamond says they want the care most of them did not get enough of in childhood. They do not want to compete for their female partner. They want to rest and relax in her love and acceptance. They don't want to have to perform or prove themselves.

It takes courage and vulnerability for a man to ask for such care in a sexual experience. They fear rejection. They fear being seen as unmanly or childlike. The truth is some women do have a hard time accepting a man who is not acting like a traditional male. We women have our conditioning too. A man who acts like a little boy in our arms may turn us off. We may fear the retaliation anger or irritability that may come later when our man feels ashamed of his vulnerability and tries to reclaim his "manhood". Or maybe, just maybe, we have enough empathy and understanding to honor our man's vulnerability with nurturing love. Maybe we have the strength and maturity to let the vulnerability transform into deep intimacy.

Unfortunately, Dr. Diamond's article only spoke in reference to heterosexual relationships, but marriage and family therapist, Dr. Kathleen Ritter writes in her article, "Therapeutic Issues for Same Sex Couples," that same sex couples share many commonalities with heterosexual couples. They struggle with developmental stage differences as when one partner begins to grow personally and the other sees this as abandonment. As with heterosexual couples, differences in desire for independence and intimacy also arise. It should be noted though that the need for a safe harbor and closeness may be amplified in a same sex relationship if their external support system—family, religion, coworkers—alienate them because of their sexual preferences.

EMPATHY

Roots of Empathy (school-based parenting centers focused on working with teen parents) founder Mary Gordon believes successful people develop empathy from receiving empathy or witnessing empathy. The essence of empathy is to put ourselves in someone else's shoes and feel what it's like there. Empathy also involves making something better for someone if "standing in their shoes" is a painful experience. In short, we try to see and feel the world from someone else's perspective. Sympathy is different. To sympathize means to stay in our own perspective but still feel for another, possibly even enough to help them. With empathy, we feel sorry with someone, with sympathy we feel sorry for him or her. Empathy requires experience and is a lifelong learning process based on relational interactions.

THE OXYTOCIN CONNECTION

Oxytocin is released when a mother nurtures a baby or when anyone works to form a kind and trusting connection. It creates feelings of calm and closeness. Oxytocin's chemistry is essential to empathy. Oxytocin increases empathy but feelings of empathy also increase the release of oxytocin!

As mentioned in Practice Two, oxytocin enhances our feelings about close relationships based on our relationships with our parents. If our relationship with our parents was difficult, we will have a tendency to react negatively to close relationships. This can be improved by rebuilding positive neural circuits through warm social contact and increasing oxytocin production.

Various forms of touching: massages, long hugs, orgasms, handshakes, and petting animals all enhance oxytocin production. Trusting, being trusted, and feeling safe emotionally with another person also releases oxytocin. Eye gazing also boosts the calming hormone.

EMPATHIC LISTENING

According to Stephen Covey, next to physical survival, the biggest human need is psychological survival—to be understood, affirmed, validated, and appreciated. Covey said one way to achieve that level of psychological affirmation and appreciation is through empathic listening. He described empathic listening as listening to get inside another person's frame of reference and really understand how they feel. Empathic listening uses our ears, eyes, hearts, intuition, and senses. We listen for feeling and meaning. We listen to make our partner feel heard and calm their nervous system.

Often when we communicate with others we seek first to be understood. We make judgments right away about the other person's contribution and when we respond we color our responses with our own autobiography. Empathic listening seeks to avoid all of that.

Empathic listening does not include:

Probing
Making judgments
Advising
Interpreting or diagnosing

Empathic listening does include:

Repeating what our partner says
Rephrasing what our partner says
Relaying our understanding of the feelings our partner conveyed

Below is an example of an empathic conversation:

Husband: I had the worst day at work. I did not get one break and my boss was on a rampage.
Wife: You didn't get a break today and your boss was on a rampage?
Husband: Yes, it was non-stop all day and I felt pressured by Mr. Rockefeller.
Wife: So, you were working hard all day with Mr. Rockefeller breathing down your neck.
Husband: Yeah, my brain is mush. I can't wait to sit down and relax.
Wife: You're exhausted?
Husband: Definitely. I dread going back tomorrow.
Wife: Sounds like you had an awful, draining day at work and you're not looking forward to tomorrow.

There is a difference between active listening and empathic listening. Active listening has the intent to use the information gathered to get the speaker to reach a conclusion. We listen and reflect but we plan to use the information to make a judgment or give advice in a roundabout way, by asking questions until the speaker comes to a solution. Active listening is often used in therapeutic settings.

Writer and creator of website comfortableconversation.com, Bennett Garner, says introverts can escape "small talk purgatory" by asking a question about something the other person said that we found intriguing. Then ask a follow-up question to that question to take the conversation deeper. Then deliver a sentence that starts with, "That must have been..." and finish it with a feeling like exciting, disappointing, wonderful, etc. This shows we were listening to the person's story and are attempting to understand how they felt. The back and forth engagement should make us both feel more at ease.

Listening with the intent to understand makes a conversation transformational versus merely transactional. At the end of the conversation, the other person feels heard and is apt to share more in the future because listening to understand and gain clarity builds trust and empathy (which aids in the release of oxytocin— woohoo!).

LISTENING DEEPLY MAKES US VULNERABLE

Listening so openly leaves us vulnerable to other's influence. For some people, this feels like giving up control, and it scares them. In studies done regarding empathy, it was discovered that over empathizing could backfire as well. For example, one study found the most empathetic nurses were likely to avoid dying patients early in their nursing training. They eventually learned to deal with the stress of empathizing with terminal patients, but initially it caused avoidance.

Potential negative influence and over empathizing are why we need a solid foundation of self-awareness, self-respect, and self-discipline. With such a foundation, we are less likely to be swayed in a negative direction. We maintain our authenticity within a relationship—interdependence.

RESPONSIVENESS

In *Born for Love: Why Empathy Is Essential—and Endangered*, Maia Szalavitz (co-author of *The Boy Who Was Raised as a Dog*, a book based on work with maltreated children) and Dr. Bruce Perry (senior fellow of the Child Trauma Academy and co-author with Ms.

Szalavitz on *The Boy Who Was Raised as a Dog*) note that from the start of life, we require others to help us cope with stress. Our brains require social experience to develop properly: we influence each other's ability to manage stress in real measurable ways. The connections are part of the architecture of our nervous systems.

As we saw in the section on attachment theory in Practice Five, the interactions with our primary caregiver as a child affect our relational abilities later in life. Those early interactions affect our ability to empathize and emote. Normal parent/child relationships provide small, manageable doses of stress in a pattern that creates resilience. The parent allows the low-level distress, such as stepping out of sight for a few minutes, but then reliably returns so the child gains confidence in her mother's return and her own ability to be alone. Consistency and responsiveness are required to regulate stress and train our brains to trust and use healthy relationships to soothe us.

One area I've put extra effort into improving is my level of responsiveness. In everything from replying to text messages to helping with household tasks, I've tried to not put others off. I realize it is not a good idea to give away all of our personal energy, therefore it has been a learning curve trying to find the proper balance between other and self-nurturing.

I find myself offering to help my kids with homework versus just telling them to do it. I try not to complain too much when they need an overnight bag dropped off at ten o'clock at night for a last-minute sleepover, but I also make it known that the respectful thing would have been to let me know earlier in the evening. I stop working when my kids get home from school and meet them in the kitchen for end-of-day connection. My aim is to deliver emotional presence with actual help.

RESPONSIVENESS A FORM OF SELF-DISCIPLINE?

I strive to be helpful to my friends and partner when they are in need. I don't ask them if they need help. They will most likely say no. I offer specific help and then follow through. I learned to do this from my former mother-in-law and an old boyfriend. They were excellent at jumping in and helping others. Their superb self-discipline did not allow them to hesitate. I still hesitate sometimes, but not as often.

It seems strange to think of being responsive to relationships as a form of self-discipline but it is a narrowing of focus (renouncing other opportunities based on what I value most) and a commitment. I consider consistent responding a meaningful practice I want to maintain.

I take note when my partner seems stressed and I offer a hug, loving touch, or warm smile. I work to create emotional connection, pay attention and respond competently, which are Dr. John Bowlby's most important emotional skills for parents based on years of attachment studies. A lot of the adult maturation process seems to be about re-parenting our partners and ourselves.

Being there consistently for a partner builds trust, strong positive chemical and physiological reactions in our bodies, and feelings of comfort and satisfaction.

STRONG PEOPLE TAKE CARE OF THINGS

Yet, it is hard and at times disappointing to expect the same level of responsiveness in return. Over the years, starting when I was a child, I learned not to burden others with my needs or feelings. Other people are busy with their own to-do lists. Strong people don't need comforting. Strong people take care of things on their own.

PERMISSION TO LET SOMEONE HELP US

In *Love and War in Intimate Relationships*, Dr. Stan Tatkin and Dr. Marion Solomon stress the importance of interactive regulation. Interactive regulation is the process where at least two individuals co-manage and balance nervous system arousal in real-time.

Often as adults we put out fires for our coworkers, resolve problems for our children, care for our aging parents, make sure our house is in order, etc. We put our partner and/or ourselves at the bottom of the care list.

WHEN WE CAN'T ASK FOR HELP

Responses learned in childhood (due to a caregiver's lack of attentiveness) and efforts to spare our partner added grief, often cause us to self-soothe or auto-regulate. If there is no spouse or partner, auto-regulation is even more likely.

When I don't have a partner to comfort me and make me feel secure, auto-regulation becomes my norm. I calm my nervous system by giving myself space and time away from the demands of others. When I don't have this time away, I get overwhelmed and dysregulated.

WHEN WE RECEIVE HELP

There have been periods in my life when a partner and I interactively regulated each other (although we had no idea we were doing that). We quieted each other's anxieties. We were a team. Those were times of wonderful inner and outer peace. For example, when hosting dinners at my house, I often get a little keyed up about making sure everything goes as planned. I've had partners who have calmed me by offering lots of reassurance and assistance. This put the guests at ease too.

Interactive regulation and attunement (a feeling of being on the same page, in alignment) produce a sense of safety and security as well as attraction.

REGULATING THE REGULATOR

My ex-husband and I had a difficult time regulating each other while disciplining our children. I would often struggle to get our kids to pick up their toys. If I happened to be having an especially hard time and resorted to yelling while my husband was home, he would come charging into the room, yell and discipline the kids with punishments (usually taking something beloved away). I assume my loud voice felt like a distress signal or he could not stand hearing the chaos and had a compulsion to settle things. Either way, it was disempowering to me and did not change the behavior of the children. The next day a similar situation would occur.

A more positive interactive regulation would have been my husband calmly entering the room, kissing me on the head and asking if there is anything he could do to help. Those gestures would have soothed our children and me as well. Kids feel secure when their parents act calmly as a team. Dr. Tatkin calls this kind of interaction "regulating the regulator." It puts our partner and our relationship first. It makes our partner feel secure and cared for.

HEALING OLD WOUNDS

Interactive regulation involves learning each other's old wounds and working to heal them. It requires closeness and keen observation of facial expressions, tone of voice, body language, etc. It requires deep listening with intent to understand the type of comforting our partner needs. It requires appreciation, respect, and admission of vulnerability.

One of my old wounds is not feeling I can count on the support of a loved one. Any sign someone is not consistently reliable with his or her words and actions, puts my nervous system on alert.

The holidays are a time when I feel that wound. I feel alone in my preparations for them and sometimes even in the celebrations. My extended family lives far away. The interdependence of a partnership has been rare in the past. It's not my children's place to provide emotional support.

My friends fill in as family and support, which I greatly appreciate. They respond to my calls. Help me put up Christmas lights.

Check on me via texts and phone calls. The inclusion of a church community has also eased my dis-ease. Knowing there is somewhere I am consistently embraced and included gives me energy to support others.

I am extremely grateful for the good people in my life who interactively regulate with me. I look forward to getting better at caring for others while being cared for.

MASTERING LOVE

In a quote from *The Atlantic* article "Masters of Love", expert in marital enhancement Dr. John Gottman mentioned two requirements for a master (versus disaster) relationship:

1. **Responsiveness.** Master partners scan the environment and their partner for things to appreciate and say thank you for versus finding things to criticize. They "turn toward" their partner when the partner sends out a request (bid) for a response. Example: If a husband says, "Look there's a beautiful goldfinch in the yard," a responsive wife would turn and make a positive, supportive comment about the goldfinch. The finch is not all that important but the response to the husband's request for connection is.

2. **Assumption our partner has good intentions.** Disaster couples take everything personally, feeling their partner is intentionally trying to hurt or anger them. Master couples assume the best of their partners. Example: Husband leaves his dirty socks on the floor. A disaster wife assumes her husband doesn't respect her and isn't considerate. Master wife assumes her husband is a little absent-minded and busy and must have missed the socks when picking up his laundry.

Both requirements lead to a sense of calm and ease between partners during peaceful times and when the couple is in conflict.

RESPONSIVENESS AND CONFLICT

As mentioned in Practice Five, responsiveness plays a significant role in conflict resolution. Instead of listening to our beloved during a disagreement with the intent to state our own case, judge them, or defend ourselves, it is more productive to listen with the intent to understand (empathic listening) and then respond to what they said, not what we want them to know about us. It shifts the mood of the disagreement. Rather than create defensiveness it creates understanding and openness to mutual resolution—a sense of "I hear you and we're in this together"—which calms each partner's nervous system.

WHY WE NEED RESPONSIVENESS

Besides other key relationships (namely children), things like work, scheduling, technology, pets, shopping, pornography, drinking, etc. can come between our intimate partner and us. It's up to us to find ways to care for our significant other and steady their nervous system.

LET'S MEET IN BED

Think back to when you were ten years old or younger. Did someone put you to bed at night? Did they read to you? Tuck you in? Talk over your day with you? Or were you responsible for falling asleep on your own? Did you read to yourself? Watch television? Count sheep? Some of your replies may give you a good picture of your caregiver's level of attentiveness and help you figure out your attachment style.

How, if at all, is your bedtime routine similar to the one you had as a young person? How is it different? Is one better than the other? Would you like to change the one you have now? Does your partner go to bed at the same time you do?

If we are a person sensitive to threats to a relationship or feelings of abandonment, the sight or feeling of an empty bed when our partner could or should be there is disconcerting even if it is on a subconscious level. Secure individuals feel the absence of a partner when they do not join them in bed too.

Our nervous systems prefer to have the reassurance of knowing someone is there with us throughout the night. I've experienced a feeling of dread and emptiness when my partner gets up to go to the bathroom and does not return right away. I can't rest easy until he returns.

One soothing ritual to maintain with your loved one is to make sure to end the day together in bed. Get ready for bed together and at least touch base physically or verbally before going to sleep. One of you may stay up later than the other but spend time together before the early bird goes to sleep. If you have to be away from the bed for part of the night, touch your partner gently when you return. Let them know you are there.

DAYTIME CONNECTION

The summer after I graduated from college I was a "summer girl" (not a very PC title) in Winnetka, Illinois, a suburb on the north side of Chicago. A summer girl was the title they used instead of nanny. The couple I worked for was a bright, warm loving pair—Mr. and Mrs. C.—with two young daughters. The couple had a genuine affection for each other I admired. Every day in the afternoon, Mr. C would call to check in with Mrs. C. He wanted to see how everyone was doing. Occasionally, we would miss his call and he would leave a message on the answering machine. I remember he always closed his message with the phrase, "Big kiss, bye!" It was so original and endearing. It stuck with me. Having a daily call or text with a loving message is a great way to make your partner feel cared for and reassured. If you can have a signature phrase or closing note, bonus points!

LEAVE ON A HIGH NOTE

I have a desire to make sure my kids always leave for school on a positive note. I try to end the night the same way. I want them to feel optimistic and loved. I have failed or forgotten many times but if I do it 80% of the time I consider myself successful. At night, I remind them of something to look forward to tomorrow. There have been a few times when I've gotten ready for bed, crawled into bed and then crawled out of bed to go deliver a caring goodnight to one of my children.

I suggest treating your spouse or partner the same way. In my marriage, I put more effort into being responsive to my children than my husband. It should be more equal or even lean heavy toward the partner. If Mom and Dad are happy, the children feel secure and happy too. Mom and Dad have more energy to devote to the family.

I knew my husband needed the warmth of my love before he left for the day and when he returned at night. I could feel his need. I just could not give it to him. Perhaps because it felt inauthentic or perhaps I felt like I lost too much of myself by pouring love on him. Perhaps my emotional connection well was too empty to offer secure affection and attention. Whatever the reason, it didn't happen and our relationship suffered for it.

As introverts, we are always mindful of energy levels. It may seem like extra work to give our partner such support, especially after we've doled out lots of attention to children, but the returns are tenfold. Caring for our spouse gives them energy to care for us.

We might also want to consider kissing our partner before they leave for the day because a study done in Germany in the 1980s showed that men who kissed their wives goodbye in the morning lived on average, five years longer and made 20-30% more income than their non-kissed peers. The kiss was not the determining factor for the results but the positive attitude the kissers started their day with, was thought to lead to a healthier lifestyle.

We all have a need to make and continuously re-make secure connections with our most important people. Daily rituals and routines make it easy to touch base with our relationship and create that safe harbor.

RESONANCE

Another valuable trait of healthy, secure relationships is resonance.

Daniel Seigel, in *The Mindful Therapist*, calls resonance "the alignment of two autonomous beings into an interdependent and functional whole as each person influences the internal state of the other."

Resonance is the ability to feel synchronized and in tune with another person. In simpler terms, it means we "get" each other. That feeling someone knows us or is inside our hearts and minds is not just magic. It's neurological. There is a mirroring system of neural circuits throughout our brains that allows us to mimic internally what is going on inside or outside someone else. The classic example is if we ask a friend to rub their hands together quickly to generate friction and heat while we watch, chances are as her hands heat up, so do ours. Within our brain certain neurons fire that allow us to feel a real but less intense version of her heat -generating action. We do that with emotions (compassion and empathy are great examples), thoughts (we complete people's sentences in our heads) and physical movement too (the friction experiment).

In a world that perpetuates the importance of boundaries, independence and competition, resonance and mirroring grant us connection.

SIGNS OF A RESONANT RELATIONSHIP ACCORDING TO DR. AMY BANKS

- We sense how our partner feels

- Our partner senses how we feel

- We have more clarity about ourselves with this person

- We "get" each other

- Our feelings impact our partner

EARLY EXPERIENCE WITH MIRRORING

If we were raised with healthy primary relationships and have experienced mature secure adult relationships, resonance is positive and easy. If our past relationships involved unsafe, unreliable or unskilled partners, resonance is more challenging. Our brain processes may not be developed or may have developed incorrectly.

If our parents were largely absent or unavailable when we were children, we did not have anyone to help us develop our mirroring practices. Looking into another person's eyes stimulates mirroring. When a parent holds a baby, and talks to them while looking into their face, the parent is encouraging the mirroring process (empathy too). Neural pathways are established. Inside the infant's brain they are copying the parent's smile, facial movements and vocal sounds. The parent sees the child and reacts to his face and coos.

LACK OF MIRRORING OPPORTUNITIES

When I was a Guardian Ad Litem (court appointed special advocate for children who are removed from their homes due to abuse or neglect), I attended a seminar where Dr. Bruce Perry (author and neuroscientist mentioned above) spoke. Dr. Perry had worked with the children from the Waco, Texas Branch Davidian sect after their removal from the cult-like environment. In fact, Dr. Perry has worked with many children subjected to gross maltreatment. For more information, I suggest reading his book, *The Boy Who Was Raised as a Dog.*

During the seminar, Dr. Perry spoke about mirroring and attachment. I was fascinated and moved then and that was ten years ago. I'm still fascinated and moved. I remember him saying it takes hundreds or even thousands of responsive repetitions to re-wire a child's brain to form mirroring pathways, particularly if the child is over three years old. He spoke of one amazing caregiver in a foster home-like setting who lovingly spent hours (hundreds) rocking and looking into the eyes of a fairly grown boy. He was possibly nine years old or older and had never had anyone connect with him like that. No one had truly seen or understood him and mirrored him in their eyes. He struggled with empathy and understanding others and because of it often lashed out in frustration. She gave the boy a chance at connecting with others, at having meaningful relationships.

MIRRORING FEAR OR ANGER

It is possible to have the opportunity to mirror someone but that mirroring could be a negative experience. A child or adult could spend lots of time within a relationship where another person mirrors fear, anger and irritability. We still mimic those facial movements, tones of voice and subsequent emotions inside of us. The neural pathways for fear, anger and irritation get reinforced. In this case, it is not uncommon for a person in this situation to over-read or become hyper-sensitized to small facial or bodily movements or tone of voice that signal imminent scary emotions or behavior. Such mirroring does not make for a relaxed nervous system. It creates a hypervigilant, stressed-out one.

CORRECTING MIRRORING DEFICIENCIES

The good news is we have neural plasticity and the ability to change our brains even into adulthood. In their psycho-biologically based book on relationships, *A General Theory of Love*, doctors Thomas Lewis, Fari Amini, and Richard Lannon cite research that suggests within relationships, limbic resonance actually revises damaged subcortical structures.

Unfortunately, the correction of such hyper-vigilance or insufficient mirroring skills still takes hundreds or thousands of hours of repetition and re-wiring within healthy relationships.

The first thing to do is spend more time with people who see us for who we are and who express emotions readily and less time with those who do not. In healthy relationships, the expression of emotions deepens the relationship, even if the emotions are not always positive. This improves our ability to hear the other person's experience. According to psychiatrist Jean Baker Miller, a key component to a growth-fostering relationship is that it produces a clearer sense of us, of others and of the relationship.

Naming an emotion we see expressed by a loved one is a good way to check in and see if we are reading them correctly. This strengthens the mirroring/resonance pathway as well. As you may recall, naming emotions is also a good way to give us a sense of control and comfort, as it is a process primarily done in the more evolved part of our brain, versus the more primitive impulsive part.

Reducing our exposure to violent images is another easy way to strengthen our resonant pathways. Seeing a lot of horrible violence and not truly being able to feel for the victims or share emotions with them is confusing to our neurological processes.

Lastly, but just as important, as adults it is valuable to be aware of our attachment style and relationship history. We are destined to repeat our old relationship patterns because we choose people who feel familiar, even if it is a bad familiar. Please remember every person is different. Just because your partner reminds you of your father when he clenches his jaw and shortens his words, does not mean he is going to explode with anger like your father used to. Knowing our patterns helps us read people more correctly. It enhances understanding and ultimately leads to more relaxed, resonant relationships.

HOW I HONED MY RELATIONSHIP RESONANCE

During the last few years of my marriage, I started a new tradition. I took one of my children with me to visit my parents in Michigan every few months. I would leave the other two kids with their dad. I missed my family and craved time in a quieter, slower-paced environment. The country setting of my childhood home and my parents' laid-back style called to me. What I did not know at the time was I was really craving a place where I was understood and seen, where my emotions and personality traits (quirks?) were known.

Each trip ended up being time with close old friends and late nights talking with my dad and stepmother. There was lots of face-to-face time and oodles of mirroring opportunities for my child and me. All kinds of emotions were expressed, but mostly happiness and joy.

I talked openly with my family about the marital strife my husband and I were experiencing. My family "got" me. They sensed how I was feeling and felt bad we were going through such stressful times. Back at home, my husband and I rarely expressed emotions, other than frustration and silent despair. We rarely had face-to-face, meaningful conversations. I missed his emotional cues and he missed mine. I found out at the end of our marriage that my husband went through a very dark time when he changed jobs. He never voiced his pain. I thought he was OK. I did not check in with him. I did not nurture him. We did not even fight or argue to give us a chance to work things through. We just went along with no resonance. I did not feel connected or heard. I assume he did not either.

After my trips to Michigan, I always felt buoyed. I had more energy. I felt like myself again. I had been seen and understood. I believe ultimately, those visits, my guitar teacher and writing groups provided enough mirroring to show me how much was missing in my marriage.

WHEN THE ALLOSTATIC LOAD IS TOO GREAT

Wondering what allostatic load is? It is the price we pay for constantly adapting to stress to maintain stability. Bruce McEwen and Teresa Seeman seem to be the lead scientific experts on it.

Arousal states (not talking about sexual arousal here) fluctuate throughout the day for each of us. Our nervous system continuously adjusts how calm or excited we are. As mentioned earlier, I've known I have a highly sensitive nervous system for years. I am easily aroused both internally and externally. I find emotions very arousing for example, as well as interruptions while I work. Introverts constantly reconcile their inner worlds with the outer world, to keep our arousal levels low. Too much noise, action or interaction ups our arousal levels internally. The constant reconciling depletes our energy.

If our partner in a romantic relationship has completely different arousal levels than us, it can cause stress and increase our allostatic load. For example, someone who loves to have the windows open in the winter and never sits down is going to clash with someone who loves to sit under a blanket near a fire reading. Their arousal levels are different. It does not mean the relationship cannot work. It simply means there will be more adjusting and experiencing of stress.

A partner who frequently yells is going to affect the arousal levels of their partner, depending on their innate and experiential relationship with yelling. Someone from a large raucous family may not mind the yelling as much as someone from a small family with serene habits.

These are two relatively innocuous examples. It gets trickier when emotions and attachment styles get involved. A partner, who trips our fear of abandonment frequently without soothing us, is going to raise our arousal and stress levels to unhealthy degrees.

If asked to adapt too often and too much and stress is prolonged, the effects on an individual's health can be extensive, even deadly. Unchecked stress can cause an abnormal or diminished release of hormonal and neurological mediating chemicals such as cortisol and adrenal steroids. Stress caused by exercise, excitement or protective impulses can be beneficial. Not all stress is bad. But, stress over a long period of time wears us down physiologically. We may be constantly fatigued, develop high blood pressure, reduced memory or even increase the chances of autoimmune or inflammatory disorders.[6]

It is essential for partners to learn to soothe, rather than threaten or negatively arouse each other.

I have had clients who, based on their health and overall negative impact on each other, needed to end their relationships. The allostatic load was just too great.

SOCIAL CONTACT AND STRESS

Throughout our lives, we need social contact to help us regulate our distress. As mentioned in the Independence section of this book, we can exercise, meditate, read or work alone to calm ourselves. Solitude is even a proven way to alleviate stress caused by relationships. But, the absence of any close human connections— non-social stress relief—rarely sustains good health.

A study reported in *The 100 Simple Secrets of Happy People* concluded that 70% of our happiness is based on our relationships. The closer ones we have the happier we are. Consider prisoners in solitary confinement. The average person can become depressed and even psychotic if isolated for just a few days. Holding hands with a loved one or even seeing their face can lower blood pressure and levels of stress hormones.

Introverts can still rejoice. We are fully capable of close relationships while maintaining our introverted nature. This is the interdependence this book hopes to encourage. If we understand and apply the awareness, calming and growing practices described in the Independent portion of this book and add the abilities to argue productively and soothe a partner, then we have the tools to create a full, rich life.

CHALLENGES TO CALMING EACH OTHER'S NERVOUS SYSTEMS

We are distressed and triggering each other's old wounds.

Action steps for soothing a partner:

1. Decide which partner is most secure at the moment. They set aside their issues and become the soother.

2. Based on your partner's preferences, choose whether to soothe with verbal or non-verbal assurances.

3. The soother acts quickly and gives positive reassurance right away. Example: (using a verbal reassurance) "I want to work through this until we both feel satisfied. "

4. Use touch, a hug, eye contact, or physical closeness if your partner is most reassured by non-verbal contact. Use heartfelt words and affirmations to comfort your partner if they prefer verbal soothing. Example: "I love you now and I will love you when we get through this obstacle."

Society wants us to be independent and take care of ourselves. The general belief is that depending on another person is unhealthy and weak.

Arguments demonstrating interdependence are the better way to decrease personal distress:

1. Note our brains have built in mirroring systems that allow us to mimic other's actions and feelings.

2. According to studies, 70% of our personal happiness comes from close relationships.

3. The production of the hormone oxytocin during bonding moments between lovers, parents and children, pet owners and pets, etc., creates a sense of calm and promotes empathy.

We don't feel heard, understood or close to our partner.

Action steps for increasing connection and resonance:

1. Boost empathy through oxytocin production. Increase production of oxytocin by touching your partner through massages, long hugs, and handholding or by having orgasms (preferably together). Even petting animals can increase oxytocin production in humans. Eye gazing is another way to create oxytocin and connection.

2. Use empathic listening to understand what your partner is feeling. Do not probe for information. Do not judge or advise. Simply rephrase what your partner says and verbalize the emotions you heard in your partner's answers.

3. Create a safe environment where emotions are valued and respected. Shared emotions and vulnerability deepen a relationship.

4. When a partner bids for your attention respond quickly. Turn toward them or move toward them and demonstrate presence. Look for ways to appreciate and express gratitude for your relationship.

5. Assume your partner has good intentions and give them the benefit of the doubt more often than criticizing them.

Partner stresses us out to the point of ruining our health. Arousal levels are too high for too long.

Action steps for mitigating allostatic overload:

1. Reduce contact with your partner if he or she is not willing to learn soothing techniques and demonstrate responsiveness.

2. Increase time with safe and nourishing relationships.

Practice Seven: Valuing Community Principles of Unity and Collaboration

As mentioned in the beginning of this book, I grew up in a small, idyllic town in the middle of Michigan. The name of my hometown is Alma which, interestingly, means soul in Spanish.

Alma in the 1970s and 80s was a homogeneous rural little berg economically supported primarily by a petroleum refinery, tool and dye manufacturer and local farming. The population hovered around 10,000.

THERE WERE DIFFERENCES BUT NOT A LOT OF COMPETITION

The inhabitants of Alma were almost all white. I remember Mexican families being the only minority. There was some prejudice. I recall hearing the terms "spics" and "pickle pickers" tossed around occasionally when referring to Mexicans. I also remember my best friend's dad being upset when she wanted to date a Mexican boy. She was a white Catholic girl from an upper-middle-class family. The boy ended up being our star football player and I believe he attended Harvard after high school.... Despite my friend's father's hesitation, white kids dated Mexican kids in high school quite often.

Religious practices were predominantly Christian. There was a fairly even mix of Catholic and Protestant. I attended mass with my Catholic friends as much, if not more, than I attended Protestant services with my family. I only remember two Jewish families in Alma my whole childhood. My classmates and I learned what dreidels and matzah were from those two families. One of the Jewish families drove a Volvo, which at that time in Michigan, was a novelty. I remember one of my snarky male classmates calling the Volvo a "Jew Car". That registers as divisive now, but I honestly do not remember any other intolerance shown toward the Jewish families. I am sure there were incidents of intolerance and misunderstanding, but to my knowledge they were kept to a minimum.

Financially, there were known differences in status. The doctors, lawyers, funeral home owners, manufacturing plant executives, and large-scale farmers were the wealthy ones of Alma. Although, we all knew whose families had money, in reality there was not much financial difference between the rich families and the poor families. The majority of us were in the middle.

My family did not discuss money at home. I knew my father was in a lot of debt, but it was OK because he "owned" shoe stores. We had something to claim as ours. Ownership of businesses allowed us the illusion of having money. My mom made sure my sister and I dressed well, another illusion perpetuating a middle-class status. I knew we did not have as much money as my friends' families (mostly manufacturing plant owners and accountants) and this embarrassed me sometimes but, overall, I felt like I fit in well with the crowd.

EDUCATION AND CAMARADERIE

There was a small liberal arts college in Alma, which not only brought a fairly educated workforce to the area but also supported our local economy. There were three elementary schools, one middle school and one high school in Alma. My graduating class had around 230 students. I could name 90% of them at the time of graduation, plus many other students in lower grades. We had AP classes—three or four of them. Our high school offered Spanish and French language classes. Despite the district's small size, I feel like we received a decent education. The teachers cared. Many of them were the parents of classmates. Many of them were friends of the community. They participated in events to promote our town, like parades and chamber of commerce events.

We often had assemblies in school where the teachers and students participated in funny, self-deprecating skits. We could laugh at ourselves. There was a good amount of pride. I do not remember a lot of competition for grades or extra-curricular activities. There was some rivalry for boyfriends or girlfriends. The dating pool was not that big. Speaking of pools, we had a pool in our high school and a good-sized marching band. I was a flag girl, pom-pom girl, and clarinet player. We had swimming, baseball, basketball, football, golf, volleyball, softball, and tennis teams. My sister played softball, volleyball, and basketball.

WE GOT TOGETHER FREQUENTLY

We had a lot of unifying events in Alma. Every Memorial weekend we hosted a Scottish event called Highland Festival. There was a parade, which all the local merchants participated in as well as all of the local marching bands. There were floats, beauty queens, tractors, fire trucks, clowns, Kiwanis, and Shriners. Kids clamored for the candy thrown from the popular floats. We all got teary-eyed when the bagpipes marched by playing their haunting tunes. During the day, Scottish games were played and bagpipe bands competed. Each night of the festival included a beer tent for gathering with your chums. Beer and bagpipes, a comforting combination. Makes me nostalgic thinking about it. I'm happy to say, all of these events still take place.

On most Friday nights throughout the school year, there was a high school football or basketball game to attend. A large portion of the community attended those games. It was a social event. The games were where we met up with our friends and families at the end of the week. They were where we cheered on our home team.

Within our families, we ate dinner together most nights. We hung out with our friends, often walking home together after school or getting together on weekends to hang out, play cards or watch movies in someone's basement. There was a lot of bike riding (and later driving) to the arcade and 7-11. I remember constantly conversing with my friends. If we weren't together we were on the phone chatting about school, boys, clothing, our families, etc.

SLOW PACE ENCOURAGES THOUGHTFULNESS?

I am not sure if there were a higher number of introverts in my hometown. I know there were extroverts, but it seemed like there was a lot of inner-world contemplating and reflective/creative thinking and expression. Perhaps the slower pace of the rural setting encouraged such reflection and respect for each other's thoughts. There was time to be thoughtful in all senses of the word.

I could be romanticizing my hometown, but I felt a tremendous amount of support and cohesion within our community. Everyone knew everyone. We worked and played together. The pace was slower and we took time to be with each other. When the massive snow and ice storms raged (and they did back then) neighbors would stop by on snowmobiles and ask if we needed anything from the grocery store. We helped each other. We needed each other to make our town run. There was a pride and sense of "we're in this together."

My Alma classmates and I still cheer each other on through social media. I'm even connected to some of my former teachers, including my kindergarten teacher. There is still a feeling of solidarity.

Does hearing about my hometown community and childhood years bring back memories for you? To clarify your original sense of community ask yourself these questions:

What was the ethnic makeup of the place you spent the most time in while growing up?

Was there a big or small difference between the wealthiest and poorest people in the community?

What did everyone do for fun in your hometown?

Was there more competition or collaboration in your primary
childhood community?

Did you feel supported and/or like you belonged in
your community?

ICELANDIC WARMTH

In *Born for Love*, Dr. Bruce Perry and Maia Szalavitz describe the
country of Iceland in surprisingly similar ways. In 2009, Iceland
had a lot of social capital. Social capital according to Perry
and Szalavitz is the economic value associated with people's
connections with and trust in one another and their capacity to form
and utilize networks of those contacts. If members of a community
know and respect each other—even those beyond their immediate
family—they are more likely to do business with each other. For
example, a farmer may be willing to buy a tractor from someone he
does not know because his cousin recommended the tractor retailer.
There is a high level of trust and a belief that most people are part
of "us," not a rival tribe. Commerce flows because of the high trust
and high levels of empathy. In places with high social capital there
is less crime and higher measured levels of life satisfaction.

Iceland, because of its harsh weather conditions and isolated
location, requires a good amount of cooperation among its
inhabitants. Family members are close and get together often.
There is very little economic inequality. Ninety-three percent
of the population is Icelandic. It is a racially and religiously
homogeneous culture.

The lack of diversity could be detrimental in some ways but in studies it has been shown to increase empathy among members. It's easier to empathize with someone who looks like you and who could be family. It also decreases the chances of "us versus them" mentality. There literally is no "them". In Iceland, people outside an individual's family and circle of friends are still trusted because they are essentially still on the same team. Same harsh weather to battle, same socioeconomic level, same ethnicity, and similar appearance. This feeling of being in the same boat, explains why people of Iceland do not mind spending money on things like paid family leave and universal health care. It helps them and their fellow brethren.

Recall our mention of mirroring in Practice Six? Mirroring systems in our brain help us connect and resonate with others by allowing us to faintly mimic within our minds what someone else is doing and feeling. It is easier to copy a reflection that looks like us with a similar background.

Guess what else increases with trust and empathy? Oxytocin! Our old friend that helps bond parents to children, lover to lover, and friend to friend by associating a feeling of safety and comfort with the other person. This same hormone also shows up when two people trust each other during business transactions. The more oxytocin we share with others, the less stress we feel and the lower our allostatic load.

I want to emphasize the importance of positive social contact. It reduces stress, which improves our health, well-being, longevity and financial status.

WHAT ABOUT THE INTROVERT WHO DOES NOT WANT SOCIAL OBLIGATIONS?

Some of you might feel uneasy about a couple of the above statements. First of all, as an introvert and someone who desires alone time, you might worry that you will have to change your nature to live a fulfilling life. Surrounding yourself with many relationships sounds overwhelming. Trust me when I say, I absolutely understand your hesitation. I have had the same thoughts.

The truth is positive relationships do not deplete us. They energize us. They bring about synergy, creating an outcome that is greater than the sum of its parts. The support of positive relationships allows us to do more than we could on our own. They help our bodies create calming oxytocin and motivating dopamine. We do not have to be friends with everyone, but studies show the more close-relationships we have the greater our chances for happiness.

Our earlier references to attachment styles and nervous system relief show that it is easier to establish positive relationships when we know our own attachment history and how to modulate it. Knowledge of attachment styles and aspects of responsive and resonant behavior help us keep calm and understanding within our relationships. They also help keep our partners calm and content. Those who chronically negatively affect our nervous systems, without any hope of reparation, do not offer the kind of social contact that is sustainable.

I am not recommending we throw our introverted traits to the wind and lose ourselves in every social engagement we encounter. The concept of interdependence still reigns. Maintaining our authentic introspective nature within positive relationships is the ultimate goal. We may need to ask for time to ourselves within our social groups.

Respectful friends, partners and associates understand our needs and do not take our desire for solitude personally. As a respectful friend, partner, and associate we reassure our mates we will return in a timely manner with more energy to support the relationship.

THAT'S NOT HOW WE DO IT IN THE U.S.

Many of you also may be thinking, but the United States is the melting pot of the world. We are built on racial, ethnic, and religious diversity. True, yet Dr. Perry and Ms. Szalavitz say historically we have been a nation with high levels of trust of outsiders and we have shown excellent economic growth. Perry and Szalavitz say a sense of similarity and at least the appearance of equality of opportunity are key reasons we have succeeded economically. Belief in the American Dream and the ability to make it big no matter who we are if we work hard, has allowed us to see all Americans as "us."

It has also been vital to keep the financial distance between the rich and the poor small. Those with similar socioeconomic status have a lot in common. They shop in the same stores, travel to the same places. live in similar homes, etc. It is easier to empathize with someone whose life is similar to ours.

Dr. Perry and Ms. Szalavitz wrote *Born for Love* in 2009. The social climate has evolved since then. The 2016 election of a president who represents a wealthy lifestyle and conservative government spending on social welfare, enables (or facilitates) a culture that seems poised to maximize the chasm between rich and poor. This is bad news for connections and calm nervous systems. According to Perry and Szalavitz, a market economy where people are obsessed with gaining wealth and possessions tends to undermine trust and increase cheating. The meritocratic focus on achievement and performance fosters competition and puts a dent in trust, collaboration and empathy.

A move toward character versus competition is needed now. Generating trust among a community's members creates oxytocin within our bodies and empathy within our hearts. Trust is built by following through on promises and consistently choosing the high road. Relying on each other and working around common ethical values joins people in secure relationships despite cultural differences, just as belief in the "American Dream" and the perceived equality of opportunity for U.S. citizens helped us maintain a high level of trust among ourselves and with foreign traders in the past.

TRADING COZY FOR COMPARISONS

Despite the cozy and collaborative environment of Alma, I was determined to get out of the small town. I was eager to become worldly. I thought success meant financial rewards, cosmopolitan experiences and something bigger than what was available in a small rural town. I also had a desire to get away from the competitive and at times, contentious relationship I had with my sister. I wanted to be my own person, with no comparisons or sharing of resources with her. I had learned to be fairly independent. I wanted to continue that trajectory.

I headed off to one of the biggest universities in the country, Michigan State University. I think it's safe to say my interest in novelty and opportunities outweighed my fear of not knowing anyone and having to meet new people. In a way, the size of the school allowed for a certain amount of anonymity. I could get lost in the large class sizes (up to 800 students per class). I could walk across the vast campus without recognizing anyone.

True to my wishes, it was a whole new experience with not much in common with my hometown. Socioeconomic status was noted and obvious based on the town or suburb you hailed from. No one had heard of Alma. Most of the people on my dorm floor, including my roommate, were from affluent Detroit suburbs.

Every ethnicity known to man existed at MSU. One I found particularly intriguing was the Jewish population. Most Jewish students lived in one or two of the oldest dorms on campus. The girls dressed differently (high pony tails, plaid shirts, tapered jeans, big boots) and there was always something labeled Kosher in the cafeteria for the Jewish students. As I said, we only had a maximum of two Jewish families in Alma at any one time. Those families, for the most part, assimilated with the Christians who monopolized Alma.

In a school with 50,000 students it is necessary to fight for resources. I had to stand in line at ungodly hours for crazy lengths of time to receive financial aid, register for classes and get food in the cafeteria. Parking spots were scarce and parking tickets were aplenty. I rarely developed relationships with professors. I figured they would never remember me from their class and it would be difficult to schedule an appointment given all of the students requesting them. Plus, talking to strangers of authority seemed daunting, a trait of social anxiety many introverts may recognize.

Whenever I met people for the first time they asked where I was from. It immediately set up "us versus them" dynamics. Since no one knew Alma, I often started out as a "them" in their eyes. They were often from the Detroit suburbs or bigger cities, like Lansing or Grand Rapids. They were already worldly. I was small-town.

Another difference I noticed while at MSU was the breadth of recreational chemicals used while partying. In Alma, alcohol was the main source of intoxication. Marijuana occasionally surfaced but mostly only stoners did that. In college, pot, mushrooms, acid and even cocaine, although still behind alcohol in usage, were much more prevalent.

I went to school using grants, scholarships and financial aid. It seemed most of the other students' parents had saved for their education. I am probably exaggerating the number of kids with college funds, but it felt like I was in the poor minority.

SOCIALIZING AMONG THE MASSES

I made friends with people on my floor and brother floor. The university was good about creating opportunities to mix socially. This was both good and bad for this, at the time, closeted introvert. My roommate was an effervescent blonde who could not wait to join a sorority. We got along surprisingly well until our sophomore year when I found a boyfriend and she joined a sorority. Prior to that she had lots of friends on campus and always knew of parties to attend. I got sick of the "Where are you from?" question and the "Are you in a sorority?" question but overall, I had a good time socializing. Again, I could maintain a level of anonymity or do what introverts do best, meet people on the fringe of the party. I could strike up a conversation with one or two people observing the action from the edges of the room. I could even join in the main activities if I'd had a drink or two. Yes, the studies correlating social anxiety and alcohol consumption ring true to me.

I also met people at my campus job at the language lab. I handed out tapes to students taking foreign language classes. Sometimes the students requested English tapes, because they were from other countries like Somalia and Ethiopia. We lab workers smugly called these students (behind their backs) J.O.B.s. ("Just Off the Boats). I'm embarrassed to admit that, but it is the truth. The offensive nickname subconsciously unified us geeky lab workers and made me feel like I fit in with my coworkers.

As you can see, there were many more instances of "us versus them" mentality. I only made one new deep friendship while I was there—Debbi. She later became my post-college roommate and longtime friend. I did date one man for a year and a half, and I met my future husband my senior year. My junior and senior year in college I had the perfect roommate—one of my best friends from Alma, Emilie. There was something so comforting and lovely about rooming with someone who knew where I came from. We never argued. We talked a lot. We had fun together. We partied the same—which was to say we liked to be social but not the life of the party. We shopped the same. We even had similar energy levels. Emilie was good for my nervous system. I think I was good for hers too.

The comfort and pleasure I found in Emilie's presence had to do with two things. One, she had introverted tendencies too. We loved doing things one-on-one, like running to discount clothing stores and looking for bargains together. She was a quiet studier and dedicated to her schoolwork, as was I. She had a calm nature, but still could get into giggling and laughing fits as we shared stories.

Secondly, she was a familiar haven in the first years away from home. The large university did not provide a lot of emotional familiarity and comfort, but it did feed my need to learn and experience new things. There is a natural pull toward the familiar and safe when we are away from our comfort zone. With Emilie, I did not experience any social anxiety. I could be myself because we were old friends. I had more courage to explore and take part in new activities because of her safe presence. Just like the secure babies with their attentive mothers in Mary Ainsworth's attachment style experiment, I felt safe and assured to explore and then return to my friend's companionship.

DIFFERENCES IN A ROMANTIC RELATIONSHIP

As I mentioned, I met my future husband my senior year at Michigan State in a business law class. He offered me a ride to class. I thought he was rather arrogant at first, because he seemed to talk a lot and brag. Bragging was frowned upon where I came from. I did not know it then but that boasting and speaking with conviction were forms of competing. It gave him an aggressive edge. It also could have been distancing behavior (avoidant attachment style) or his way of trying to impress me.

We came from very different socioeconomic backgrounds and he was Jewish. He grew up in a mid-sized city in Ohio. His father was a surgeon. His parents were still married and they had his college and graduate school financially covered.

Although scientific evidence says we are attracted to what is familiar, I seemed to be attracted to novelty and differences. Perhaps I was subconsciously looking for a relationship like the one I had with my sister, so I could heal it?

Nevertheless, we fell in love. I adored his stories about his active, close-knit family. He made me laugh. I appreciated his intelligence and sense of security.

We dated for six months at MSU, and then broke up when we graduated. We were rather practical about it, but I did feel a loss. He had a job lined up in Ohio. I had plans to move to Chicago. Yes, I wanted to move to an even bigger arena with even more diversity. I believed success looked like people who lived in big cities. They seemed so smart, independent, efficient, and worldly. If I could make it there, I would be impressive.

I lived on saltine crackers and peanut butter dinners, but I made it there. I lived in the city with Debbi, the one new close friend I made at MSU. She was from a smallish town in Michigan with a similar upbringing to mine. We held our small-town values but explored and experienced every inch of the big city. I gathered knowledge of people and places. I picked up a few skills to advance my career, such as Excel spreadsheet manipulations and office diplomacy. All of it aimed at advancing my status.

Eventually, my husband and I reconnected and got married. We moved five times after we were married. Each time living in or near a large city. I worked outside the home until our oldest son was born in Houston, then I stayed home with him and later his brother and sister. I made a circle of friends in each place we lived. Even as an introvert, I wanted regular connection and engagement. I constantly reached out to or was approached by new people. We maintained a decent balance of social and downtime. My husband liked just having time with the family. I enjoyed that too. The addition of our daughter, giving us three children four years old and younger, made downtime almost impossible. Then we moved to Minneapolis.

LIFE IN THE BIG LEAGUES

My husband received a job offer we could not refuse, even though my initial reaction to Minneapolis was, "No. I don't know anyone and it's a tundra." He would work for a promising hedge fund. During the interview process, the company wined and dined us. We had a personal assistant who stood at the end of the restaurant table, explaining each of the six to nine courses we received. We learned proper wine pairings and what an amuse bouche was (a single bite-sized hors d'oeuvre served for free to patrons at the chef's discretion). I can't lie. I loved it and found it fascinating. It satisfied my needs for novelty and impressiveness.

We picked up stakes in Ohio (leaving behind good friends, a wonderful college student who helped weekly with the kids, and a comfortable middle-class lifestyle) and moved to the suburbs of Minneapolis. Our children were five, three and one at the time.

We left our 1970s-colonial home in Ohio for an early-2000s build in Minnesota. We had ten-foot ceilings, five bathrooms, five bedrooms, a movie theater and an exercise room. I was so excited to move into that house.

Neither my husband nor I had any family in the area. We had no babysitters or friends either. My husband went to work at his high-paying, high-pressure job every day. I stayed home with the kids.

"An isolated mother is a distressed mother." — **Dr. Bruce Perry**

A TRIBE WOULD BE NICE

In *Born for Love: Why Empathy is Essential—and Endangered*, Dr. Bruce Perry and Maia Szalavitz state that humans have spent most of the last 150,000 years living in multi-generational, multi-family groups. The ratio of mature individuals to young children in these clans was roughly 4:1. An abundance of kin surrounded kids and helped educate, nurture, discipline and enrich them.

Now the average household has 3.53 people (2016, per The Statistics Portal) and teachers are outnumbered 30:1 in classrooms (2010 census). We have created a much more isolated culture where extended family does not even live in the same state, let alone the same house.

As an introvert, I am not sure I would love having a twenty-person clan around all the time, but I definitely see the benefits of multiple nurturing bonds for my family and myself.

Soon after our move to Minneapolis is when I found myself in the doctor's office asking for a pill to give me energy, a sex drive and a mood boost.

In *Wired to Connect*, Dr. Amy Banks states that when we are cut off from others, our neural pathways suffer and this can result in chronic irritability, anger, depression, addiction, and physical illness. The human brain is built to operate within a network of caring human relationships. To reach our personal and professional best we must be warmly and safely connected to partners, friends, coworkers, and family. Within such relationships, our neural pathways get the stimulation they need to make our brains calmer, more tolerant, resonant, and productive.

In the suburbs, there were few unifying events. There was a monthly Bunco (dice game) night for the neighborhood women for a while. I met a few women there, but everyone seemed focused on their kids and running a household. Wealthy lives are complicated. Everything from home decorating to child presentation to fitness and appearance must be perfect. With all that money, it is expected everything be done to the hilt. We did not help each other a lot either. Everyone relied on family or managed their household by themselves.

We did not cultivate a religious practice or membership to a church or temple. I was not 100% sold on Judaism, and my husband was not interested in anything to do with Christianity. We did not celebrate Christmas. We did celebrate Passover, but most of the time by ourselves with no extended family present.

There was little time for casual socializing. It was rare for my husband and I to get invited to events outside of the occasional office party.

I know, I know. Cry me a river. It is hard to garner sympathy when you seemingly have everything, but there was a feeling of emptiness. I felt alone but also overwhelmed by family and obligations. I could not articulate the alone feelings until years later.

FINDING SUPPORT OUTSIDE THE MARRIAGE

I did make friends at the gym. The health club offered a bright spot and good opportunity for social interaction. They had childcare, which my kids did not like. I felt guilty for putting them in childcare but it was the only nourishing grownup time I had.

I later started taking guitar lessons and writing classes. These fed me, but took me further away from my marriage and at times, my children.

Our marriage started to unravel. My husband and I were not a team. We did not shore each other up. We did not agree on disciplining the kids. We did not offer each other compassion or presence. Passion was nonexistent. At times, I did not feel we were even friends. I believe we mostly saw each other as resources. It was lonely.

During the next four years, my husband made the most money he'd ever made and lost his job. Neither brought us together. We did the obligatory counseling but we could not fix the marriage. We divorced after four years of treading water.

The next two years I focused on taking care of my children, building a business, and dating. I leaned on my writing group friends for emotional support. We met weekly for a while but then reduced our meetings to monthly. I talked with my parents via phone regularly. They were wonderful sounding boards and gave me a lot of beautiful emotional validation and support.

I realize the gym and taking classes might not be the right fit socially, financially, or schedule-wise for everyone.

To find your right fit, I suggest reflecting on the times when you feel most alive.

When do you feel at home?

When are you most energized?

Those places and people are the ones who can heal you. If you do not have a rejuvenating place or person in your life currently, think about when you were younger.

What or who made your eyes sparkle in the past?

How can you connect with something similar now?

For example, if when you were younger you loved to play school with your siblings, see if there is a way you can get involved with a local school. Could you volunteer? Could you get a job there? Do you know any teachers you could kindle a friendship with?

If you have a major interest in something like teaching, astronomy, knitting, or whatever, the list is endless and the Internet is your friend. Search for online groups with the same interest. Although it is comfortable and convenient to only convene online, I highly recommend finding a group that meets regularly in person. The in-person meeting offers more neurological and social benefits, including an improved ability to read facial and body language cues. In-person relating is ideal, but online social groups are still beneficial to banishing the feeling of being alone.

THE TRIBE GETS SMALLER, BUT THE WORKLOAD REMAINS THE SAME

I felt relief after the dissolution of the marriage. Not having to face a sad marriage every day lightened my spirit for a while. But then, the heavy load of managing a household, raising kids, and building a career from scratch without emotional support hit me.

Children do not understand the full weight of a parent's workload, but they have an uncanny way of noticing what is different and what they are missing. They definitely do not know the emotional toll of a bad relationship or a workload for two that one person now handles. I did not want them to know, so I tried to keep it all together myself.

That community tribe sounded better and better.

FORCED COLLABORATION

Two years after the divorce, my mother was diagnosed with a form of ALS or Lou Gehrig's disease. She still lived in Alma, Michigan. She never remarried after my parents divorced. She was single, and needed my sister and me to help her. The type of ALS she had affected her cranial region first. Her speech deteriorated right away. Within months of noticing a slight slur, she could not make any voluntary movement with her mouth or face. We could no longer talk on the phone. Along with her speech, her ability to swallow declined. She went from being a meat and potatoes lover to a ramen soup eater to taking in packaged formula through a feeding tube.

She moved in with my sister and her family for about six weeks. My sister lived an hour away from Alma. My mom did not want to leave Alma, but she was not healthy enough to live on her own. It was too hard for my sister and her family to care for Mom daily. My sister was a dentist, and her husband was an assistant professor at a major university.

Beside the medical care Mom needed, she also suffered greatly psychologically. She had lost her home, her ability to talk, and her ability to eat. She could not be left alone, or she would panic. We moved Mom into an assisted living facility. It was difficult for her to make friends there, as she could not talk and did not join the others in the dining room because it was torture for her to watch others eat regular food. She refused to learn how to type and use a keyboard for speech. Even with those barriers, two female residents did approach and befriend her. God bless them.

I flew back and forth to Michigan as often as possible. I visited every six to eight weeks for a long weekend. During my visits, I stayed with my sister and her family. Twenty-six years of living apart and the necessity to work together for the good of our mom's care helped eliminate residual tension between my sister and me. My brother-in-law also served as an excellent diplomat and buffer for two sisters with different personalities.

NOT SO DIFFERENT

Surprisingly, when we were together, my sister and I discovered we were actually quite alike. We are driven, creative, curious, and have a love of personal development. We see the possibilities and believe in relationships.

During those visits, I spent time with my sister, her husband, my niece and nephew, and, of course, our mom. I felt a sense of being a part of a family. The reason for my visit was painful, but the healing and unity that came out of those times fortified my nervous system. It was profound to be part of such a team. I think my sister and brother-in-law felt the same way. My sister and I no longer competed; we collaborated and supported each other.

Our mom died two years after her diagnosis. At her memorial service, a childhood friend of hers told us stories of how popular our mom was and how she thrived in her childhood hometown—a small town where her family owned a hardware business. She had many friends and boyfriends as a young person. Her older siblings teased and nurtured her in fun, lively ways. She belonged to a nice community. She was happy there.

Spending time with my mom at the end of her life, made me realize how isolated and alone she had been for decades. Her siblings were much older and lived far away. She never remarried. Her parents had been gone since I was nine and my sister and I had moved on with our own lives and families. Her nervous system was on high alert and never calm. She did not have many nourishing relationships to ease her mind and spirit. She never wanted to leave Alma. It was the only community she had left.

HOME AGAIN

Less than a year after my mom died and a month after the breakup of a long-term romantic relationship, I was at loose ends. I felt untethered. I had very little sense of belonging to anything. My short list of close relationships was shorter. The kids were with their dad half the time, and my friends were busy with their own lives. I was hesitant to get back into the dating world so soon after the breakup. I needed time to process and do a postmortem analysis.

I started a search for a spiritual community. That realm of my life had been vacant for decades. I had done lots of reading on different spiritual topics such as meditation and Buddhism. I practiced meditation semi-regularly. But what I longed for was an actual community.

The purpose of this section is not to proselytize or convince anyone to find spirituality or religion. It is to show the value of finding a supportive community.

One Sunday, I walked into a small church in my area. A kind gentleman greeted me and gave me a nametag—everyone wears nametags at this church. Introverts appreciate nametags, as it relieves the pressure of remembering names while being social with strangers—already a monumental undertaking for us. He directed me to the sanctuary. I found a seat on the far right, close to the piano. Several people introduced themselves and welcomed me. The minister happened to be out that particular Sunday but other congregants read poetry by Mary Oliver, played music on guitar, and gave "sermons" on living meaningfully. They opened the service by stating they are an intentionally inclusive congregation welcoming all people of good will.

By the end of the service, my nervous system rested in an amazing calm. The small congregation, with its lack of pretention and surplus of warmth and humility, felt like home.

Later, back at my house, I read the bulletin explaining the church's mission and values. This congregation finds the essence of religion in character and conduct. They "gather in community to give worth to values, interdependence, inherent worth, compassion and love." It is definitely, a collaborative versus competitive environment. Empathy and trust abound in an atmosphere of acceptance and willingness to learn about differences.

It is hard to distinguish who are the wealthy congregants. Financial status is not a factor given much thought. Values and working together are bigger focuses.

Differences in financial status or cultural background are not seen as obstacles to connection. A willingness to learn from each other and a belief in community and good character bond the congregation.

As I continue to attend today, I've noticed a feeling of increased security within myself. The church and its community are always there. Several of its members have shown considerable kindness in welcoming me to the group. I have a sense of being guided by elders, as some of the older congregants have taken me under their wings. It feels good. It helps fill the hole the loss of my mom created and the lack of family in the area perpetuates.

ENERGY SOURCE FOR THE INTROVERT

I've noted this spiritual community, like my writing group and closest friend groups, generates energy rather than depleting it. As an introvert, this boost is a vital element to my overall joy. It allows me to give back to the church and its members. I love volunteering there, even for non-fun jobs like cleaning up the kitchen. I am limited by my availability, but not by my energy or desire to offer help to this community.

All the good will and good energy of the congregation is supported by the structure of regular meeting times and rituals (candle lighting, singing certain songs, coffee and cake after services).

In many ways, the church community reminds me of my hometown and the feelings of safety and comfort I associate with it.

Interestingly, I learned of this fitting spiritual community through my sister. She and her family attend the same denomination of church where they live.

CHALLENGES TO SECURE COMMUNITY BUILDING

Our culture has made it easier to feel isolated. We are a transient population. Fewer people live near family. Busy schedules prevent community gathering. Technology encourages virtual connecting rather than face-to-face meetings. Ironically, we seek humanity through machinery. So many differences between people culturally, financially, and philosophically make it difficult to create community. We are taught independence is ideal. Dependency is weak.

Action steps for creating community

1. Generate empathy by finding common values and increasing trust. Focus on character versus competition or comparison. More empathy equals more bonding oxytocin. The globalization of our world makes diversity the norm. Instead of emphasizing differences in an us versus them scenario, appreciate differences and allow them to enrich our lives. Focus on commonalities like the human search for connection and security. Different cultures may have different traditions but we all have traditions.

2. Minimize financial inequality or at least the perception of financial inequality. Teach values that emphasize humility and discourage flashiness. Keep talk of personal wealth to

a minimum by focusing on topics showcasing hard work, compassion, and willingness to learn.

3. Emphasize education and growth over success and material wealth. If we are all learning, we are all winning. An openness to learn new things from each other maximizes synergy. For example, encourage questions from all family members at the dinner table. No question is too silly.

4. Allow different generations to mingle in projects together. Let children see how adults are humans who laugh at themselves. Let children see how adults value hard work and community. Emphasize how we contribute instead of how we win.

5. Make helping others in the community a common practice. Just as my childhood neighbors offered to get groceries for us during a snowstorm, we can all extend a hand to help strengthen the ties of community members. Times of adversity, although difficult to endure, often provide the perfect opportunity to create unity.

6. When looking for a community, search for one that meets regularly. Consistent meet-up times and dates create routine. Routine provides the structure a community thrives on. For example, friends who share a devotion to a certain sports team know they can count on seeing or talking to each other on game day.

SECTION IV: BALANCE AND FLUIDITY

In the previous sections we learned the different perspectives and dynamics needed to achieve dependence, independence and interdependence. Each type of interpersonal relating has its appropriate situations. Moving from a predominantly dependent to interdependent lifestyle demonstrates a progression in experience and maturity. No longer depending on others' approval for our personal evolution is a sign of growth. Learning to know ourselves—both our shadow and sunny sides—and practicing self-discipline and self-regulation give us the confidence to self-express and enter high-quality relationships. Being able to maintain our personal integrity within a loving and healthy relationship is also a sign of growth.

This next and concluding section has to do with moving fluidly in and out of all three of the previously discussed levels of dependence or independence. It is not an endeavor of equality. We spend disproportionate amounts of time in dependency, independence, and interdependence. The goal is to spend less time in dependency and more time in interdependence. Why? Because interdependence warmly embraces independence and dependence. Because interdependence with its elements of authenticity and relationship offers the solitude and interaction that fills our sensitive introverted human needs best. It allows us to do deep introspective work and share it with others. It allows us to self-regulate and feel the comfort of being cared for and loved.

A common assumption is that we can self-regulate or be independent and resolve our anxiety, stress, or fears entirely on our own. Psychotherapist and co-regulation specialist Bonnie

Badenoch says we can calm ourselves with self-regulation options such as meditation or solitude but they do not heal the anxiety or emotional wound. It will still exist as an undercurrent and something we repeatedly have to push down or fight. Co-regulation or dependence on a partner or companion to soothe us has the ability to heal wounds and reduce triggering effects Dr. Stan Tatkin and Dr. Amy Banks say our brains are wired to co-regulate.

Another point to consider is how effective we are at resolving issues when we are stressed. When our brains are hijacked by fear or worry, we tend to not think clearly. The most evolved and cognitively rational parts of our brains get side-stepped when processing stress or trauma. Studies show children do not learn well when an adult is yelling at them or when they are overcome with worry about an outcome. Adults are the same way. In fact, the Israeli army keeps soldiers awake and surrounded by warm social interaction after a traumatic experience because sleep tends to consolidate and ingrain the trauma. Altruistic social contact reduces the chances of developing Post-Traumatic Stress Disorder. Therefore, it is hard for us to calm ourselves when we are anxious or stressed. The comforting presence and/or actions of another are more effective.

Seeking balance between our inner and outer worlds is a tail-chasing activity. Not that it is not possible to do both; the trouble word in the above sentence is balance. In any one day, balance between our inner thoughts and the external world is unlikely. Feeling comfortable with the level of introverting and extroverting we do each day is a gift. Our ability to do concentrated work and provide focused attention on significant relationships ebbs and flows from day to day. Some days push us to a stressful imbalance where we spend too much time adapting to a highly extroverted and stimulating environment. If we are lucky enough to have solitude during working hours or in the evening and have time to collaborate with others in comfortable proportions, we are resourced to do great things.

Unfortunately, trade-offs are often the more likely scenario. We frequently miss out on one opportunity to do another. For example, television writer and producer, Shonda Rhimes (a proclaimed introvert), says in her 2014 commencement speech at Dartmouth, if she attends her daughter's debut in the school musical she misses actress Sandra Oh's last scene ever filmed on the set of her show Grey's Anatomy.

Ms. Rhimes' example is one involving two outer world activities. As an introvert, many times we have to give up alone time to join social activities. One rather personally distressing example of this is when, in the past, I had to take a day off from research or writing because my children were home from school for a snow day or minor holiday. This situation was doubly distressing because not only did I not get to make progress on my work, I felt guilty for not being excited about the time with my children. I am happy to say I have learned how to moderate the irritability I felt when I had to set work aside, and I now look forward to such days with my children. I'll explain how I learned to do this in the following chapter, Practice Eight: Honor Our Inner and Outer World.

Rigid delineation of work and family time is not always possible, as in the above example, when children are home when they would normally be at school. This last section intends to help us honor both our inner and outer realms while living in a frenetic and distracting world. As introverts and/or people with sensitive nervous systems, we do things slightly differently than our more gregarious extroverted, highly resilient brethren, but there are ways to make transitions between our comfort zones and challenge zones easier. We can move more fluidly between the two. We can learn to be more resilient.

In this section we'll talk about transcending our inhibitions about living an active social lifestyle. We'll talk about working with purpose and energy. We'll talk about leaving anxiety and emptiness behind and feeling joy and contentment instead.

Practice Eight: Honoring Our Inner and Outer World

Principles of Balance and Contentment

It is difficult when we experience a season of Giving Up. I'm not talking about Lent. I'm talking about one of those phases in which we feel defeated by the overwhelming requirements of life. It's when we find ourselves constantly giving up what makes us hop out of bed in the morning to fulfill pressing and unavoidable obligations. We don't have a choice. There's no way around the onslaught of work and needs requiring our attention. We give up because it's easier to do what's expected. We don't have the strength to handle day-to-day chaos and live vividly.

HOW TO KNOW WHEN GIVING UP HAS STRUCK

The following are a few symptoms of the dreaded season: crying in the shower, 4:00 a.m. anxiety, a sense of being trapped, lifeless eyes, and a buildup of clutter and broken things. We may think we are inoculated against its effects, but immunity is rare.

Every few months we surrender dreams, freedom, and self to reality, responsibility, and everyone else's needs. Feel fortunate if you only suffer occasionally from giving up because for some, this is a chronic condition.

We will usually feel GU coming on before it strikes. Exposure to children being home from school for extensive periods of time, home ownership headaches, frustrating work experiences, and/or endless errands and compulsory confrontations precede the very worst cases.

Succumbing to the funk, we watch passions go down the toilet. Buried under the covers of a rapid-fire existence, we beg for mercy and rest, but like all serious maladies it commands attention. Don't even think about having energy to do anything beyond have-to's. Forget reading. Forget exercising. Time to think isn't likely. Writing is out of the question. Give up the pleasing feeling of contentment. It's all about survival now.

We'll do anything to stop the onslaught of obligations and subsequent feelings of entrapment. We clear out all frivolous activities and resolve to complete the compulsory tasks. All the while praying, please don't let this last long.

THE BRIGHT SIDE

We can lie on the couch, drink ginger ale, and watch bad television, letting the housecleaning go and ignoring our buddies' calls asking us to hit the gym or go have a beer. This is great for a while, even nourishing, but make sure we don't languish there forever. Too much lounging turns to avoidance and further overwhelm. To-do lists metastasize and make it difficult to stand on our own two feet again. We could grow even wearier from lack of solitude, lack of creativity and the denial of our true self.

A positive aspect of surrendering to all that must be done, is the clarity it brings. What we ache for during those stretches of unconscious living is what we must pursue as soon as we find the strength.

REMEDIES FOR OBLIGATION OVERLOAD

Even in a weakened state, know we won't forsake being for doing forever. We will recover and find balance to our days again. Here's how:

1. **Curiosity**: Curiosity will pull us out of a stupor. It will get us talking, listening, learning. Even buried in to-do's, our antennae are up, listening for bits of fascinating material. We'll hear a book mentioned on the radio that piques our interest. Another parent will mention they just got back from Belize and we will want to learn about Belize. A child will need help with a school project and the research will inspire us. Ideas will incubate and then beg to be carried out. Our eyes will sparkle again as we engage in keen observation and poignant questioning. Our color will return. We can't stop our introverted nature from wanting to explore something in-depth. We can't stop our extroverted nature from wanting to get out in the world again.

2. **Resonance**: Just when we feel ourselves going down for the count, we throw back the curtains and let sunshine pour in in the form of hauntingly beautiful music, a shared joke or an active comment thread on a topic we adore. Knowing others feel a deep connection to something we do is a huge boost.

One person admitting to being on the same page as us is life enhancing, invigorating.

3. **Solitude**: Nothing soothes frazzled nerves faster than space or downtime. Many claim to thrive in hustle in bustle, but solitude relieves the sensitive person. It stops the bleeding. It slows the heart rate. A lack of solitude is often what causes us to give up in the first place. We feel we must cater to others. Eventually, it becomes apparent that we will not thrive if we do not get alone time.

4. **Receiving Care:** Just as it felt so good when our mom made us Jell-O and put cool compresses on our forehead, the gentle touch and soothing words of another human work miracles to heal our weary body and spirit. If there is no caregiver to comfort us, the first three remedies will serve us well, but the responsiveness of another human immediately lightens our load and completes the healing regiment. Knowing someone cares and is there to support us is a most effective balm. They can't always take over our work but they can kiss our forehead and treat the most virulent case of Giving Up by calming our nervous system.

Succumbing to too many obligations can cause an imbalance in our well-being. When we say "Yes" too often and neglect our introverted need for quiet and reflection, we put ourselves on the path toward anxiety and fatigue. Our energy flags and we are not well-resourced. We don't honor our inner world. We simply get by. We put one foot in front of the other and keep everyone else happy.

This may sound like some people's version of what we are supposed to do. We are supposed to take care of others at the expense of ourselves. And sometimes, we have no choice, but when the outer world wins over the inner world for too long, everyone suffers.

We need a balance between our inner and outer world. We need a balance between our temperament and our personality.

TEMPERAMENT OR PERSONALITY?

"Natural inclinations are assisted and reinforced by education, but they are hardly ever altered or overcome." — **Michel De Montaigne**

Psychologists say there is a difference between temperament and personality. Temperament is a series of behavioral and emotional traits we possess at birth. Personality evolves after cultural influence and experiences are added to temperament. It's the classic description of nature versus nurture.

I turned to the work of developmental psychologist Jerome Kagan to find out more about the nature aspect of introversion and high sensitivity. Kagan did a long-term study on children starting when they were four months old and ending in their adolescents. Kagan and his staff hypothesized they could predict which babies would be introverts and which would be extroverts.

In 1989, when the babies were four months old, Kagan and his fellow scientists exposed them to many different stimuli, ranging from recorded voices to popping balloons to alcohol on Q-tips. The babies' reactions were then recorded. Some babies (20%) reacted immediately and gregariously. They waved their arms and legs and cried loudly. Others (40%) remained calm and only moved their arms and legs occasionally. The remaining 40% fell in between the high-reactors (flailing limbs and crying) and the low-reactors (steady nature, minimal reaction).

Kagan predicted the highly reactive babies would become the introverted adolescents and the lower reacting babies would be the extroverts.

Flash forward eleven years. Many of the kids dubbed high-reactors were indeed more careful and serious eleven year olds. The low reactive babies were more laid back and confident.

OUR NERVOUS SYSTEMS ARE DIFFERENT

When the babies participated in the initial experiment and subsequent check-ins at age two, four, seven, and eleven, the scientists did more than just observe the children's reactions to novel stimuli. They also monitored their heart rate, blood pressure, finger temperature and other elements of their nervous systems. They measured those properties because they are indicators of responses from the amygdala in the brain. If you remember our previous discussion about the amygdala and the primitive brain, you might recall it takes in information from our senses and then tells the nervous system and rest of the brain how to react. If necessary, it sets the fight-or-flight response in motion. It is the first alert to danger.

Children with highly reactive amygdala will do what they can to minimize its reaction in the emotional controlling limbic system (part of the brain where the amygdala resides). They vigilantly search for environmental threats so they can head them off before they occur. They carefully decide whether to join new groups or explore new places, and if they do, they enter each new situation slowly. Hence, they exhibit what is traditionally thought of as introverted behavior.

Other studies based on identical twins conclude that temperament is on average about 40-50% heritable, meaning our introverted or extroverted nature is partially due to our genetics. How much genetics are responsible varies because the 40-50% heritability is an average.

Kagan even went so far as to say he saw a correlation between blue eyes, allergies, hay fever and high reactivity (ultimately introverted behavior). This correlation is not 100% accepted by other scientists, but Kagan saw a correlation.

My mother always said I was a colicky baby. I cried a lot. I was fussy. I bet I startled easily (I still do). I never liked summer camp and to this day, I enter a pool or lake very slowly. Cannonballing was never my style. I also have blue eyes and hay fever—just to add to evidence of my predisposition toward sensitivity. So, my genetic makeup is partially responsible for my introverted nature.

THE INFLUENCE OF NURTURE

As we saw in Practice Five: Opening to Conflict, our early relationships affect our way of relating within future relationships. Attachment styles develop when we're young but adjust and adapt based on the level of security we experience in our adult relationships. To decipher the genesis of our attachment style we can ask ourselves the following questions:

- Are we open to collaboration and mutuality in a romantic relationship because our primary caregiver as a child was attentive and in tune with our needs? If so, we most likely started out with a secure base and attachment style.

- Or are we averse to dependency on another and at home in autonomy because our parent was not available for us in a positive way? If so, we most likely started out with an insecure base or avoidant attachment style.

- Or lastly, are we ambivalent about intimacy—desiring it deeply one day and pushing it away the next—because our early childhood caregiver was inconsistent in their support and attentiveness? If so, we most likely started out with an insecure base or ambivalent attachment style.

It is important to mention that our primary caregivers are not solely responsible for our relationship security or lack thereof. Other adults may serve as mentors when it comes to forming relationship styles. Our parents may have been remiss in their caregiving, but a kind teacher or uncle may have stepped in to show us how a sensitive and considerate relationship looks.

Future partners can positively or negatively influence our reactions and behavior within relationships as well. Depending on their attachment style, they may help us evolve into more secure partners or more insecure ones. Our attachment style is fluid based on all of the relationships that shape us.

The rest of my behaviors and traits can most likely be attributed to the nurturing I received (or didn't receive) and the environments I encountered over my lifetime. Those traits could be called my personality.

As a child, I learned to figure out my own worries. I didn't always have or take opportunities to have my parents help with them and I certainly did not want to give my sister ammunition for teasing me. Also as a child, I learned from my father how to be curious about the world and meet new people and explore new places. When it came to emotional issues, I discerned it was safer and/or better to control them or work on them myself, but physical engagement with the outer world was encouraged.

I took this ability to emotionally self-soothe learned in childhood with me into my intimate relationships as an adult. It helped me get by when my husband was not emotionally available, but eventually my withdrawal to self-regulate caused stress on our relationship. We both needed the comfort of each other and did not have it.

My penchant for exploring had me out in the world doing new things and meeting new people, making myself happy without my husband. When I returned home, the gloom set in again.

NOURISHING THE SENSITIVE INNER REALM

To keep us on an even keel we need to nourish both our inner realm and our outer realm. We need to make sure we do not neglect one or the other, thus creating an imbalance. Our day-to-day existence may not be evenly balanced between our internal thoughts and feelings and our external relationships and environments, but over the long run, we strive to feed both.

As introverts and/or highly sensitive people, our inner worlds are our safe kingdoms. When we are mentally healthy they provide shelter, peace, and creative space. When we are struggling mentally, they can be scary places of rumination. To keep our minds healthy and minimize anxiety we need the following:

1. **Learning and reading**. Insight and understanding revitalize me. Which is why, like many introverted and introspective people, I love reading. Reading is really a search for resonance, knowledge or ideas. Reading feeds our curiosity,

as do places and people. In a way, we create relationships with books, places and people. We create lasting ties through memories, deep experiencing and connection. It is OK to let it all affect us because it provides peak understanding and perspective.

Understanding and perspective light us up. They give our lives meaning and perpetually affect us. The openness to truly understand another's viewpoint leaves us vulnerable at times. We can be influenced. But the same openness often leads to the ability to influence others. Not in a domineering way but in a two-way, win/win way.

2. Emotions. As mentioned in "Practice Two: Calming Our Nervous System", emotions are vital to our health and decision-making. If suppressed for too long, they cause damage to our cardiovascular, digestive, and immune systems. If we try to deny our emotions because somewhere along the line we perceived they make us weak, we miss out on the valuable feedback of emotions. The numbness we feel without them is a lead-in to depression. If labeled and expressed wisely, they can bring calm to our minds and bodies. Emotions tell us when we are in danger. They tell us when to run, fight and what is worth fighting for. According to David Brooks in *The Social Animal: Hidden Sources of Love, Character and Achievement*, emotions coat every decision factor, giving weight to each option and helping us make choices. If our inner realm is flooded with dark or unexpressed emotions, we struggle to make progress. If we pay attention, value and express our emotions in healthy ways then we feel competent and less stifled.

3. Solitude. Time alone relieves us of our duties to others. It lets us think and work without interruption. We can concentrate and do creative work. It allows our imagination to make its creative associations. For those who gain energy by going inside thoughts, solitude is a necessity. It is where we breathe big gulps of restorative air. It is where the flow state slips in. Ironically, it is often where we reflect on our loved ones and develop a longing for their company.

4. Low stimulation and slowing down. Our nervous systems crave gentleness. We have to escape from the rushed anxiety that is most of our days. We are often pulled through life by scheduled events, beeping alarms and the needs of others. Removing ourselves to a library, nature, our own office, or a quiet café gives us the opportunity to come back to ourselves. It lets our mind make patterns out of our thoughts. A distraction free environment like this fosters concentration and pushes our cognitive capacities to their limits, thus making us more productive, adding value to our work and making our contributions harder to replicate (i.e. have a low-experienced person or machine do it) according to Cal Newport in his book, *Deep Work*.

A slower pace also serves as a catalyst for creation. Idleness is the perfect priming of the flow and artistic pumps. Another way to calm our minds and catalyze creativity is to immerse ourselves in vastness. Studies show placing ourselves near things that make us feel small, like the ocean, a starry sky, or an open field, gives us a calming sense of being part of something bigger than ourselves. Our brains can't quite process the complexity and magnitude of such things and therefore we experience a sense of awe that enlarges our perspective.

5. Sleep. Sleep is the lowest level of stimulation. Even though our brains are quite active during sleep, especially during the REM stage, sleep remains a huge contributor to rejuvenation both physically and mentally. Although, as mentioned earlier, sleep after traumatic events is problematic in that it consolidates and ingrains the stressful memory. As was said in "Practice

Two: Calming Our Nervous System", poor sleep worsens our mood, lowers our pain threshold, and interferes with learning and memory. It deters our focus and makes us more impulsive. Lack of good sleep also affects us physically. It can increase blood pressure, elevate stress levels, and harm the immune system. It can even lead to an increased risk of drug or alcohol addiction. Introverts, with our highly reactive nervous systems, need sleep to soothe our nerves and deeply process all the stimulation we collect throughout the day. Studies have shown that introverted brains put more information into long-term memory, thus taking longer to both place and retrieve. If we do not honor our sleep needs, we have a greater risk of falling into depression, something sensitive folks are already at higher risk of developing if in stressful environments.

NOURISHING THE SOCIAL EXTERNAL REALM

We need an external expression of what goes on in our internal world to feel whole. Relationships provide that arena. Within relationships there are key elements which fuel security. They are:

1. **Responsiveness and good intentions.** Dr. John Gottman's two requirements for a master relationship from "Practice Six: Calming Each Other's Nervous Systems", are responsiveness and assumption of good intentions.

   Responsive partners scan the environment and their partner for things to be grateful for and appreciated. They turn toward and respond to their lover's bids for attention. For example, if a woman tells her husband she's had a stressful day at work, he attempts to soothe her by acknowledging her tired state and offering to make dinner and have a quiet night at home.

Responsive partners are not perfect but they are reassuring and consistent at least 80% of the time.

In a secure relationship, the partners assume they have each other's backs. They know not to take their partner's anger, mistakes or unkind words personally. Whatever happened was a temporary slip up and not an attempt to hurt or frustrate them. For example, if a wife is short with the kids and her husband at the dinner table one night, the husband knows she is not purposely trying to aggravate or hurt them. He thinks about it and remembers she did not sleep well last night and had a clash with her boss that day. He strokes her arm and kisses her on the forehead and asks if he can help her somehow—thus demonstrating responsiveness. She sighs, relaxes and apologizes for her bad mood.

2. **Understanding attachment styles.** As mentioned above in reference to nurturing, attachment styles give us our baseline method of relating. Knowing and understanding our own attachment style and those of our important people, goes a long way toward creating harmony. For example, one divorced client with an avoidant attachment style, spent nine days without seeing his children because his ex-wife took them on vacation out of the country. Initially, upon hearing of his ex-wife's plan to take the kids on vacation, he was not bothered and figured he would get extra work done in their absences. But a few days prior to their departure his kids kept telling him how much they were going to miss him while they were gone. Knowing his avoidant attachment style, and its reliance on independence and autonomy as protection from rejection, he let his kids' words sink in and allowed himself to miss them too. His children's words pointed out his true feelings, feelings he often stuffed down to avoid being hurt. He noticed the emptiness he felt when the kids were gone. Luckily, he had a responsive partner who kept him busy while his children were

out of the country. All of the awareness led to more secure functioning within his parenting and intimate relationships.

3. **Understanding the special needs of an introvert or sensitive person.** Dr. Jay Belsky, a professor and expert on child care, says that high-reactive kids (the ones in Kagan's experiments who reacted the strongest to novel stimulation) who enjoy good parenting, child care, and a stable home life tend to have fewer emotional problems and more social skills than their lower-reactive counterparts. According to Belsky, the ideal parent for a highly reactive child is: someone who can read their cues and respect their individuality; is warm and firm in placing demands on them without being harsh; promotes their curiosity, academic achievement, delayed gratification, and self-control; and is not harsh, neglectful or inconsistent. Some of those same parenting characteristics could apply to the interactions between romantic partners. Someone who both challenges and supports their loved one in a kind, sensitive way encourages the partner and the relationship to flourish.

4. **Participating in all kinds of relationships.** Children challenge us to understand different personalities and exercise patience. They teach us about secure love and its importance. Compassionate people in a spiritual community or circle of friends feed our soul. They offer support. They remind us of our true selves. Relationships with colleagues, teachers and mentors show us how to collaborate and how to learn from others on similar missions. Intimate relationships are a mix of support, challenge, and joy. They're an opportunity for emotional safety and physical intimacy, which enhances happiness. Because of their constancy and closeness, they resurrect dynamics from familial relationships. These reminders, if used wisely, can serve as opportunities to heal old wounds through reassurance and behavior counter to our past experiences.

CROSSOVER: WHERE INNER AND OUTER COLLIDE AND SYNERGIZE

"When an introvert cares about someone, she also wants contact, not so much to keep up with the events of the other person's life, but to keep up with what's inside: the evolution of ideas, values, thoughts, and feelings." —**Dr. Laurie Helgoe,** *Introvert Power: Why Your Inner Life Is Your Hidden Strength*

There are a few situations where our inner and outer worlds meld. Where they meet up and transform us. I've listed several below.

- **Healing through relationships.** As has been mentioned several times, relationships can be the crucible for healing. Because of their closeness and constancy, they trigger many of our old fears created by previous relationships, including those with our parents. The outer-world existence of our relationship triggers the inner manifestation of our fears, but the beautiful thing is the same dynamics can help us work through the old fears and wounds. Our partners or friends can provide the understanding and reassurance we did not receive previously. They can elevate our level of security by not doing what hurt us in the first place

- **Restorative narratives.** According to psychiatrist, Dr. Dan Siegel, forming coherent narratives that explain how our childhood relationships affect us now, can help us transcend insecurity. If we can see how our past wounds shaped us and influence our reactions, we have a good chance of overcoming the negative impact. If we can frame our obstacles in a positive light, all the better. For example, if we were forced to be self-reliant and autonomous as a child because our caregiver was not available, we can now view our independence and the ability to get things done as strengths that help us achieve in our career. Our career success gives us confidence, helps us maintain personal integrity and helps us handle the ups and downs of a relationship better

- **Value based work/contributing.** Valued work or as Professor Brian Little calls it in *Quiet: The Power of Introverts in a World That Can't Stop Talking, personal projects* allow us to act like extroverts. Our values are ingrained in the work, which gives us the energy to advocate and strive to accomplish an endeavor. Carl Jung, arguably the first declared introvert, did his deep work both in his stone house outside of Zurich (Bollingen) and in Zurich while seeing patients. He wrote in Bollingen and practiced psychiatry in Zurich. According to Cal Newport in his book, *Deep Work,* Jung used a bi-modal philosophy to achieve deep work. By employing solitude to tap into his inner voice while working in Bollingen and expressing and using his skills with patients, colleagues, family and friends in Zurich, he accessed both his internal and external world. Another important facet of valued work is its contribution to the greater good. It may start out as research to gain insight about ourselves, but in the end what we learn benefits more than ourselves. I know this path well. I started out getting quietly focused on reading and research to learn about my own temperament, but ended up being a voice for other sensitive individuals. My writing and personal coaching are perfect outlets for sharing what I learn and what I value (authenticity, empathy, and secure relationships). I can honestly say my work gives me energy. Deeply valued work and relationships require less adaptation and therefore do not drain us as much. I could not stop doing my work if I wanted to

- **The arts and creativity.** Acts of creativity bring the inside out. Acting, writing, painting, dancing, software design, etc, may start with outside inspiration, but they then move to the inner workings of our imagination and expand. Once an idea or project is manifested it is introduced to the outside world again. Artists often spend a lot of time alone, because it takes intense concentration to make associations and connections between items that have not been connected before. It takes quiet to hear and feel their emotions. Many creators like to hide behind their work. A scripted character is the perfect disguise for someone ordinarily uncomfortable in the spotlight. Once a project is complete, it is time for an audience. Dr. Laurie Helgoe says the expression of internal contents without interruption is a very introverted desire. It is the joining of inner and outer worlds. Authors get to spend countless hours alone working on their craft, tapping into their inner voice, but eventually share their writing with others or at the very least have a tangible piece of external work representing their thoughts

- **Movement that puts us in tune with our minds and bodies.** Yoga, running, swimming, martial arts, dancing… the list is practically endless. The key characteristic is the ability to remain self-contained while participating outwardly in the activity. It's possible to dance within a crowded club for instance, but still be deliciously in our head. Our bodies and minds are active. We exist in the inner and outer world

BEING WELL-RESOURCED

Balance and contentment come when we feel well-resourced. We are well-resourced if we feel supported in our relationships and we get enough time for restorative inner work.

If we diminish uncertainty within our relationship, we reduce the amount of energy we spend obsessing and worrying about its viability. Security frees up resources. With replenished energy, we can focus on personal development and relationship support. No one grows or learns well in a hostile, depleting environment. Always auditioning or waiting for the relationship to end exhausts us. Consistent reassurance from both partners toward each other, fills us up. Knowing there will be conflict, flaws and past baggage, but having an attitude of "We will work through everything together" allows us to relax. Accepting each other as we are is a huge energy boost.

When I was married, there was little reassurance between my husband and me. We both had our own professional and familial agendas. We had our visions and needed the other to play their role. We didn't look at each other as loving support or cherished individuals. We were resources for social and professional climbing. We were caregivers to our children but not to each other.

I made the mistake of asking for a divorce every year in the summer. I had little opportunity to self-soothe in the summer with the kids home. I needed the most comfort and emotional support from my partner during those days, but I did not know how to ask for it and he did not know how to provide it. I would rescind the request for a divorce and try to work on the marriage throughout the year, but then in the summer when my nerves were shot after having the kids home every day and no real reassurance in my husband's love for me as a person, I would ask for a divorce again. This threat to our marriage kept my husband auditioning all the time. There is no way he could have felt safe, when I had made it clear I was unhappy and had one foot out the door.

During those last few years of the marriage, it was deemed selfish of me to want to do work other than parental caregiving, spousal support, and household maintenance. Any time I dedicated to writing, learning, or volunteer work (outside of the kids' schools) was seen as time I chose to leave my family unsupported. I now understand I most likely triggered a feeling of abandonment (for my husband and my children) when I chose to do those things. That, coupled with my annual divorce request, definitely had my husband on edge. In that environment, neither of us was well-resourced.

During those years, if I had an hour or two to work on writing I was lucky. Most of my creative time was peppered with interruptions from kids, my husband, repairman, etc. I used to feel trapped. I longed for time alone. I would get angry when interrupted. I needed solitude and work time to self-regulate. I exhibited avoidantly attached characteristics. I wanted to grow and develop but I had no time or energy for it.

Now, my children are older and more independent. I have a supportive and reassuring partner. I have time during the day to devote to research, writing, and coaching. When the kids come home after school, I shut down my work. When my daughter gets home she comes into my home office and plops down in my big cozy chair, chosen specifically for its sit-down-stay-a-while design. I join my sons in the kitchen for a snack and after-school catch-up session. I turn toward them. I look into their eyes (but not too much, teens don't love that). I listen and respond to their comments. We connect through presence. The state of presence is learned. It takes effort to not allow distractions to pull us away. Responsiveness is key. When we are loved and reassured, we flourish.

BALANCE

Security and insight make transitions easier. They make us calm. I get my fill in both inner and outer arenas and therefore find it easier to move between the two.

I had to learn what to respond to, what I valued most. I do not have the time to respond deeply (as most introverts and highly sensitive people prefer) to everything. Priorities must be sorted by values. Being mindful of our allostatic load also helps. Those activities and relationships that only add to our stress and anxiety, have to be pruned. Constantly adapting or acting out of character overwhelms and exhausts us. Those experiences and relationships we find meaningful have to be developed. There is a balancing act between inner and outer satisfaction, between authenticity and relationship. The most meaningful balance derives from interdependence and the ability to move fluidly between independence and dependence.

It has been said that maturity is the balance between courage and consideration. It takes courage to assert our own perspective. It takes consideration to ask others theirs. I'm slowly learning how to create such balance. When we are surrounded by secure relationships and have time to go deeply introspective, we are full. We are balanced. We are both introvert and extrovert, but mostly we are content.

THE CHALLENGES TO HONORING OUR INNER AND OUTER WORLD

In our culture, sensitivity is often seen as weak. Honoring our desire for a calm and introspective inner state feels like we are inferior to our bolder counterparts.

According to Dr. Elaine Aron's work in the area of high sensitivity, 15-20% of the population is highly sensitive, including animal species. Recent studies show highly reactive children do worse in negative environments but better in positive or neutral ones.

Their immune systems are more resistant and levels of anxiety are lower than less reactive children when they reside in positive supportive environments.

Action steps to increase our fortitude and resilience are:

1. Seek and invest in responsive and reassuring relationships.

2. Engage in meaningful and valued work. Notice where you enter the flow state. Give yourself time to deeply concentrate by minimizing distractions.

3. Form your redemptive narrative. See how nature and nurturing influenced your temperament and personality. How did your struggles fortify you?

Quite often we find ourselves spending a majority of our time in our inner or outer world. There is an imbalance that makes us tired, overwhelmed and unfulfilled. We do not feel whole.

Action steps for managing the imbalance:

1. Realize it is OK to devote more time to one realm occasionally. There will always be trade-offs. Some days your family needs you more. Some days you need to exist in solitude to recover from over-extending yourself. The goal is a long-term overall balance.

2. Recognize the imbalance and intentionally work to restore balance. Most of the time this impulse will come naturally. Our psyche craves wholeness, as Jung pointed out. If you've been in your head thinking and thinking, make an effort to get into your body or your environment. Take a yoga class or go running (which are actually crossover activities, engaging both

your body and your spirit/mind). Which brings us to the last suggestion for restoring balance...

3. Look for crossover activities. As mentioned earlier in this chapter, activities that engage the inner and outer worlds promote bliss. You can find contentment and a feeling of balance in acts of creativity; nourishing relationships; values-based work that contributes to the greater good; restorative narratives and independent athletics.

CONCLUSION

Safe in Solitude and Relationship

The conclusion of this book includes a personal epilogue and a summary of the maturity evolution that leads to resilience and a fulfilling life for the sensitive introvert.

> *"Mary also was an accomplished ballet dancer as a child, which gave her a way to work off energy and to find a niche in which she excelled. That talent, plus being raised in what Kagan called a 'benevolent home environment,' might have helped shift Mary's innate inhibition to something more constructive. If Mary's high-reactive temperament is evident now, it comes out in the form of conscientiousness and self-control."* —**Robin Marantz Henig,** *Understanding the Anxious Mind,* **New York Times Magazine**

Some newborns have more sensitive nervous systems. They startle easily. Their heart rate shoots up and their blood pressure rises more than others when they face new situations. These are children Jerome Kagan labeled highly reactive in his experiments. We discussed these experiments earlier in Practice 8: Honoring Our Inner and Outer Worlds. Of the 20% of infants who reacted strongly from exposure to novel stimuli, only a fifth of them reacted as sharply to stressful experiences at age ten or eleven. A third of the 40% labeled low-reactives still remained especially calm. Most of the kids in the later experiment had moved toward the middle or a more moderate temperament. Almost none of the kids moved from one extreme to the other. This suggests that disposition evolves over the course of our lives depending on how outside experiences wire our brain. The range of evolution has limits based on our innate temperament. We are never going to go from highly reactive and anxious to cool as a cucumber. We may move from highly reactive to a calmer more moderate temperament.

We manage our emotions and reactions better when we are well-resourced. Well-resourced for sensitive people means we've had time to ourselves to develop self-awareness, self-discipline, and self-soothing as well as time with others to create trusting, safe, and loving relationships. Interdependence and being well-resourced go hand in hand. We arrive at interdependence by advancing along a maturity continuum.

DEVELOPING RESILIENCE AS A HIGHLY SENSITIVE AND/OR INTROVERTED PERSON

We move through the maturity continuum by passing in and out of stages of dependency and independence and ultimately landing in interdependence.

DEPENDENT

As young children we are extremely reliant or dependent on our primary caregivers, usually our parents. Ideally, they provide a deep sense of trust and safety—two cornerstones of secure attachment. They see our inborn temperaments and respond sensitively to them. Even if we are fussy or "slow to warm up" children, our parents accept us.

As I mentioned, I was a fussy, colicky baby. I depended on my mother to nurture and care for me despite all of the unpleasant crying. I am not sure how much time my mom spent talking and cuddling with me, but I am certain she took care of my basic needs. I have a feeling she was attentive as far as eye contact and talking to me. She passed away two years ago and would probably have claimed not to remember, if I had asked her; so I am left only with speculation based on her later behavior. I also believe parents were a tad more removed in the 70s than they are currently. It was, for instance, more accepted to bottle-feed than breastfeed back then. I was fed formula.

As we grow up, but remain in the dependence stage, we seek other's approval and rely on them to give us an identity based on their reactions to our behavior and temperament. We begin a search for admiration. We focus on socially approved motivations such as good grades, a large social circle, or making the cheerleading or basketball team. Later, as young adults, we may look at going to college or finding the right job post-high school. Making money and starting a family eventually creep into our identity formation. We want to belong to something and we want to fit in.

My father, again being a dad of the 70s, spent most of his time at work or out in the yard or garage. I'm not entirely certain he was even at my birth. As a young girl, I remember waiting for my dad to come home so we could have dinner. He often worked late. After my parents divorced (I was seven when they separated), I traveled back and forth between parental houses—seeing my dad on Thursday nights and every other weekend. My dad soon remarried and started another family. He also began to buy shoe stores and spend even more time at work. He paid child support and was extremely interesting and loving when he was present, but he was a busy man with lots of people depending on him. He also had passions that motivated him, such as car racing. His new wife and sons appreciated and participated in those passions. My sister and I were not as interested or involved in them. We wanted him to be involved in our interests. My sister spoke up about it, and my dad and stepmom attended most of her athletic events.

My dad gave us kids a gift in that he said "No" to us. He also taught us how to work. He showed us how to wash dishes, dust, and vacuum. I learned if I wanted personal time with him, a good way to get it was to work with him. I would go with him to one of our out-of-town show stores during a special sale day (like sidewalk days or back-to-school time) and help. We would have a good breakfast, leave early in the morning, and drive to the store. The time in the car with Dad listening to music and talking was priceless. He would point out landmarks as we drove and talk about the crops in the fields and how they were thriving or not. He'd mention people he knew or memories he had in each town or village we drove through. After a long morning of setting up and waiting on the public, he would take me to a local restaurant for lunch and introduce me to the people he knew. The long hours on my feet measuring other people's feet and selling shoes was well worth the chance to be close to Dad.

We hated Dad's distractedness and sternness at the time, but looking back I see how his work ethic, passion and ability to say "No," taught us self-discipline, self-motivation, and how to appreciate things we earned or were given.

My mother remained unmarried for the rest of her life. She was consistently there making sure food was on the table, toiletries, school supplies and that our social status remained reasonably respectable. She drove my sister and me back and forth to our friends' houses and supplied us with a car when we could drive. We had regular healthcare, hair appointments, and shopping trips. She scheduled around us.

My sister and I had a combative relationship our whole childhood. Resources were tight (money, attention, bathroom time), so we competed. We picked on each other verbally and hit each other physically. As someone with a highly reactive nervous system, it was much more comfortable to stay away from her. I would have given anything to be on the same team with her but the common belief was if we showed kindness or vulnerability the other one would use it to hurt us.

My immediate family gave me a sense of identity. At the time, it was a quiet, sensitive and slightly insecure identity. There was an inconsistent feeling of safety in my childhood homes. It was not safe when my sister was around because conflict inevitably ensued. My dad was often not available for soothing and his house had a more chaotic atmosphere because of all the people and activities. My mom was harried by life's responsibilities and lack of support. That may sound like a lot of uncertainty and insecurity, but the majority of my childhood felt safe due to my parents' overall commitment to the family and the presence of good solid friendships and wonderful grandparents. I vividly remember receiving a loopy-lettered, hand-written note from my best friend, Laura, while visiting my grandparents for a week in the summer. Laura told me everything I had missed at home and most importantly, she told me she missed me. That letter and the nurturing I received from my loving grandparents that week had my cup of security running over.

I was dependent on my family, but they were not 100% there. I did not have complete security in childhood, which is not unusual. Only a little more than 50% of us report having secure upbringings. My mom was mostly security and steadiness as a parent but not as an adult. She needed more safety and security in her life. She herself was often not well-resourced. My dad, with his doting parents (my doting grandparents), supportive wife, meaningful work, curiosity, and exciting passions, modeled a well-resourced adult.

I could not completely rely on my parents to provide financial and emotional support so I learned how to be self-reliant in those areas. I could count on myself. Thanks to my dad, I also had the sense that most people were good and will help if you ask. I had experienced the closeness and cohesiveness of a small town. I had enough intelligence and gumption (thanks to my primarily positive childhood and curiosity) to strike out into the world.

If we feel safe, it is easier to leave our secure home base and explore the world. We know we have reliable care waiting for us when we return. It is easier to move into the independent stage.

INDEPENDENT

"Two people can experience the same level of anxiety, he said, but one who has interesting work to distract her from the jittery feelings might do fine, while another who has just lost his job spends all day at home fretting and might be quicker to reach a point where the thrum becomes overwhelming. It's all in the context, the interpretation, the ability to divert your attention from the knot in your gut." **—Jerome Kagan, Psychologist**

In the independent stage, we shift our focus to an "I" driven life. We are in charge and create our own identity. We move away mentally and/or physically from our family of origin. We build trust in our own abilities through repetition, mastery, and self-discipline. We cultivate self-awareness through self-reflection and time in solitude. We seek to understand who we are and what we have to offer.

We have to learn how to calm ourselves. As dependent people, we relied solely on others to help us feel balanced and secure. As more independent individuals, we dig deep into self-awareness. Where do we feel most at home? Where do we feel most alive? What makes us anxious? What soothes our soul? Who makes our lives better? What comes easily to us?

We pay attention to our internal cues. Because we've experienced a sensitive nervous system our whole life, we develop coping mechanisms and ways to move to more moderate reactivity. We know it is more comfortable to be calm.

As introverts, we learn solitude soothes our frayed, over-socialized nerves. Solitary exercise or meditation also restore our energy. Noticing our strong emotions and labeling them allays their power.

Remembering people who offered nurturing and a calm presence in the past helps us soothe ourselves in the present.

We figure out what to do for a living and how to align it with our values and skills. We harness our ability to deeply concentrate and delve into the flow of work that includes just the right amount of challenge and skill. We express ourselves. We refine and define ourselves through self-discipline. We increase our trust in our own ability to make it in the meritocratic, careerist society.

We spearhead our lives. We collect experiences, and make ourselves more interesting and better fits for whatever environment beckons us and gives us a sense of identity.

I felt bold and independent when living in Chicago on my own after college. I saw each step, whether it was a move to a huge city or employment in corporate America, as a way to etch out my identity and make me more valued and interesting. Cosmopolitan cities and corporate work made me feel sophisticated and accepted. I had friends at work and in the city. My mom visited every few months, and we talked weekly on the phone. I had my family's moral support from back home, but mostly I was on my own. I was making my life up as I went along. I learned enough self-discipline to succeed at my job, keep my apartment clean, and get me to the gym a few times a week. Self-mastery still eluded me. I had not stumbled on what truly made me tick.

I was still dependent on society's approval. I was on my own financially and physically, but I filled emotional holes with other people's ideas. I married a good man a few years into my post-college independence phase. Even my marriage partner choice was influenced by other people's opinions. My mom's lifelong search for security from others influenced my choice of a solid, stable family man. Once in the marriage, I deferred to my husband's decision-making to set up our future lives together.

Toward the end of the marriage, I began to truly awaken and sense independence. I stopped depending on my husband to guide me and sought my own feeling of home. I began writing. I met kind, non-meritocratic friends, who liked me for me. I found independence through work I deeply valued and safe friends. I had a secure home base, from which to venture, but it was not my real home base. My marriage was not a safe place. We did not support each other and provide the kind of reassurance that makes us feel secure. Neither of us completely or consistently dropped our guard. I had learned as a child to not do that. I always worried my sister would have taken advantage of it. I subconsciously thought my husband would do the same thing.

My husband and I had strong intentions to make the kids feel safe. We put the kids and work first and each other last. Without love and reassurance, child-rearing was stressful and the marriage was empty.

I was independent but desperately wanted connection and safety.

INTERDEPENDENT

According to The New York Times columnist David Brooks, trust is habitual reciprocity that becomes coated with emotion. We slowly learn we can rely on each other through consistent communication and cooperation. As mentioned above, trust and safety are cornerstones of security.

Trust and safety within a relationship free up resources. We do not have to use energy to worry about the viability of the relationship. We do not have to worry about being judged and rejected or abandoned. We can be ourselves. Once we have an authentic identity established, we can move among all different kinds of people without feeling threatened. We become more psychically whole, as Jung said.

Later in life, toward the end of my marriage, I reached out to my dad and stepmom. They were there for me. They were tremendous emotional support as my marriage ended and my single life began. I know psychologically that did a lot for my security. My mom and I continued to talk frequently. We both needed that close connection. I felt supported.

The eventual decline of my mother's health brought my sister and me together as a team. We had to work through physical, emotional, and spiritual adversity together. I needed more time alone to process and recharge than she did. She needed more activity and interaction than I did. But that was OK. I was able to manage my emotions better than in the past. She was able to show hers more. We both had grown and changed over the years.

We both were so exhausted that our guards naturally dropped. We grew closer because of it. Vulnerability connects. We helped and collaborated with each other instead of competing. We found meaning in the obstacles.

When we are well-resourced and authentic within a relationship, we create new positive neural pathways in our brain. We can explore the world and return home to safety. In interdependence we provide security for others too.

I recently attended a birthday party for my boyfriend's father.
I enjoyed moving about the room speaking with his various
relatives—men and women of all ages, some of whom I'd never
met. Periodically, my boyfriend would join me by my side and put
his hand on my back or ask if I wanted a drink. In between talking
with others, I would join him where he was and touch his arm or
take his hand. The consistent responsiveness buoyed my social skills
and comfort. I believe I made him feel secure as well.

MATURITY

One point I would like to make is that just because we have
energy and are well-resourced, this does not mean we should do
everything presented to us. We have to make sure others, like our
children and partners, are secure too. This is a sign of maturity.
As Stephen Covey said, maturity = courage + consideration. Even
though we have the courage to be ourselves and take on new
situations, it does not mean we can neglect others.

I recently experienced a situation where I had to put this kind of
maturity into practice. I had been feeling very full and secure in my
work and relationships. I had made good progress on this book.
I felt like I was serving my clients well. My partner and I were
deepening our relationship and my relationships with my children
felt solid.

My church came to me and asked me to consider sitting on the
board of trustees. My initial reaction was to leap at the opportunity.
I wanted to give back to the church and I love that kind of visionary
work. I looked into the actual hours of commitment that came with
the position. It was a three-year commitment. I would have to switch
parenting nights (complicated) with my ex-husband to avoid conflict

with the church board monthly meeting. I have a college tour or two with my oldest son planned for the upcoming year. My daughter's dance class is on the meeting night. I wanted to give the church my dedicated attention in that role as well.

In the end, I decided to keep the kids' schedule stable and uncomplicated. I considered the position, my family, and my energy levels (still an introvert). I decided the mature thing would be to decline. I can do it in later years when the kids are gone.

I have finally found a balance between my inner life and my outer relationships. I have found and made relationships my sensitivity can rest in. They provide reassurance and the proper challenges to make me grow. The secret and missing piece for me was to let my partner, kids and clients rest and feel safe too. Gaining that wisdom moved me a little closer to maturity. I still have so much to learn and practice.

The above is my redemptive or restorative narrative. It is how I reconcile my past with my present and create a coherent story that influences my future in a positive way. I use the story to see the pattern of struggle and harmony, struggle and harmony. I see the benefits of learning from past wounds. I feel more secure in my ability to survive the obstacles in relationships and cultivate a safe harbor for my companions.

My hope is that the eight practices in this book help you develop your own redemptive story. May they also help you find and create safety and trust within relationships.

ACKNOWLEDGEMENTS

Many special people made this book possible. I am forever grateful.

To Bryce, Josh, and Anna for our lively kitchen discussions and your honest feedback. I love you and your beautiful different perspectives.

To Mom, I wish you were here to see this. Thank you for your consistent love, care, and devotion. It made me stronger.

To Dad and Jan, for showing me life's an adventure you must embrace. Also thank you for providing emotional support and a relaxing place to retreat to when life gets overwhelming.

To Jeff, for teaching me so many things, from financial responsibility to the importance of family connection. I learned many things from our relationship. Thank you. Thank you also for being a consistent and loving father to our children.

To Lisa, for challenging me, being an inspiration for this book, and the great friend Grandma K. always said you'd be.

To Mark, for your enthusiasm and support. I rest and recharge in your reassurance. You're the best, truly.

To Hugo, part for being a non-intimidating but discerning and motivating editor. Your comments and suggestions provided the perfect feedback. Thank you for pushing me just the right amount.

To Michael D., Mike G. and Roxanne S. thank you for championing me. You started the ball rolling.

To Brenda Ueland, although you've left this Earth, your writing continues to inspire. It changed me.

To my loving and supportive readers, you make all the difference. Your responses fill me up and make me feel like I belong. Your understanding is priceless. You inspire me. I hope to give as much to you.

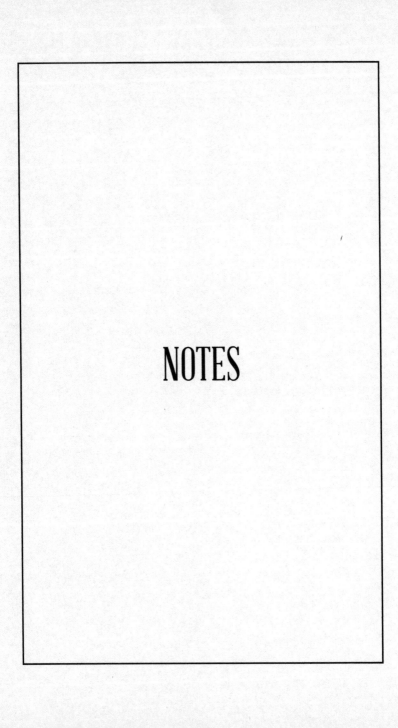

NOTES

1. "How Can You Tell If You Have Anxiety?", Quickanddirtytips.com, Robert Lamberts, MD, accessed May 15, 2017, http://www.quickanddirtytips.com/health-fitness/mens-health/how-can-you-tell-if-you-have-anxiety.

2. Dr. Alex Korb, *The Upward Spiral,* (Oakland, CA, New Harbinger Publications, Inc., 2015), 164.

3. David Janowsky, Shirley Morter, and Liyi Hong, "Relationship of Myers–Briggs Type Indicator Personality Characteristics Yo Suicidality In Affective Disorder Patients," September 11, 2001.

4. P.L. Graves, C.B. Thomas, and L.A. Mead, "Familial and Psychological Predictors of Cancer," *Cancer Detection and Prevention* 15, no. 1 (1991): 59-64.

5. T.E. Seeman and S. I. Syme, "Social Networks and Coronary Artery Disease: A Comparison of Structure and Function of Social Relations as Predictors of Disease," *Psychosomatic Medicine* 49, no. 4 (1987): 341-54.

6. Truity Dyometrics.